T0407469

GARDENS FOR MODERN HOUSES

GARDENS FOR MODERN HOUSES

Design Inspiration for Home Landscapes

BETH DUNLOP

CONTENTS

INTRODUCTION
THE MIDCENTURY GARDEN, THEN AND NOW

The decades after World War II transformed the way we live, moving America—and Americans—from city to suburb, creating not just new social mores but an entirely new landscape aesthetic. There were new roads, new jobs, new cars, and of course, with that came new houses, most of them in the suburbs. The postwar modern house and its setting offered a new paradigm: a different way of looking at the way to live that was at once pragmatic and creative, one that linked architecture and nature, taking the built world outside and bringing the garden into the house. To wit, the garden became part of the house and the house part of the garden, creating layers of looking and layers of living.

The modern house was in many ways the harbinger of the enormous and eventually tumultuous social and cultural change that was to follow, as a newly affluent and newly mobile middle class emerged. The promise of a new carefree lifestyle that came with the millions of new postwar houses permeated the American consciousness through magazine articles, advertisements, and of course on the newest of path to persuasion, the television. Historians would balk at portraying those years as idyllic, because they were not, unless you looked at them through the filter of Madison Avenue, the fictions of the Cleaver family, or the brilliant but seductive lens of Julius Shulman's camera. Along the way, of course, there were important modern houses with important modern gardens—landscapes that changed design history.

In those postwar years, Americans spilled into the suburbs, moving into Cape Cods and colonials, of course, but also into split-levels, ranches, and prefabs. Returning veterans who had been barracked in such cities as Miami or Los Angeles had gotten a taste of endless summer and the promise of a more casual lifestyle led the march to sunnier spots where there was room to grow. Many, most, were new homeowners—thanks to the Veterans Administration's easily mortgaged, if often modest, suburban houses and opportunities for education and employment—and newly part of a burgeoning middle class.

Temptation and promise came in the form of sprawling new neighborhoods and planned subdivisions and more, in houses from William Levitt, Alexander Homes, Joseph Eichler, Don Scholz and numerous others. The idea of the modern midcentury house was honed and refined in such developments as Hollin Hills, Arapahoe Acres, Paradise Palms, and more. It was not just a place to live; it was the American Dream.

The house, mostly, was simple, a straightforward "machine for living" (a phrase adopted from Le Corbusier and widely adapted and applied). And the garden was the picture-perfect outdoor component of it all. There were porches and patios, and there were pools, all of which gave rise to a new backyard culture—a world of barbecues and tether ball poles, chaise lounges for sunning and patio sets for poolside cocktails, and an easy-to-assemble aluminum Christmas tree for the holidays.

More than a half-century later, Americans are ever-more house proud, and despite the almost irreversible march toward bigness—after more than three decades of land-gobbling, space-stealing McMansions usurping our neighborhoods—there is a renewed interest in the smaller, simpler houses of the postwar suburbs, and with that the landscape that accompanied them. In this post-millennial era of Pinterest and Instagram, alluring images abound, bringing with them a new generation of buyers and near-cult-like devotion.

The social and historical (and psychological) legacy of that era is still being examined more than a half-century later, but the legacies of landscape design and architecture, for some years overlooked, are now well celebrated—and are being reinterpreted afresh by a new generation of landscape architects, architects, designers, and homeowners.

As it was then, so it is now: often, the midcentury house is a blank canvas—simple, minimal, and aimed at easy living but built without frills. In those early days, some (though few) new developments had memorable settings. A handful boasted big-name landscape designers who created the streetscape, the parks and public spaces. Joseph Eichler's name today is almost synonymous with the image of the cool, mod, midcentury home, but generally (there were exceptions) Eichler turned the houses he built over to the buyers without any landscaping at all, leaving homeowners to their own imaginations. The sparse yards of many East Coast developments, such as the many Levittowns, have been well documented by sociologists, historians, artists, and filmmakers who show the ways in which homeowners adapted, changed, ornamented, gussied up, and otherwise personalized their lookalike houses.

Then as now, modern landscape design is ever evolving, varying from region to region as garden-makers grapple with site, orientation, topography, climate, rainfall, and more. But now as did then, certain principles prevailed.

In the midcentury garden, geometry did not necessarily have a formal rigidity, symmetry was optional (and asymmetry was modern, like jazz), and biomorphic curves led to a seductive landscape. The main goals of the modern garden for the modern house were the essential ones: to unify house and garden both visually and physically, to create outdoor rooms, and to minimize maintenance and maximize the aesthetics—whether it was seasonal (as it was in much of the northern two-thirds of the country) or potentially year-round.

Of course, there were, and still are, variations on the theme: tropical (wet) gardens, desert (dry) gardens, rigidly geometric gardens, soft-edge biomorphic gardens, western gardens influenced by the rugged landscape, eastern gardens guided by the Zen principles of Japanese design, coastal gardens, woodland gardens. There were decks, porches, patios, and of course pools—a great postwar innovation for the middle class. Modern furniture was widely available, well promoted, and often surprisingly affordable. It was after all, the era of good design for all.

THE FAB FOUR

Both the modern house and the modern garden sprang from a deeper and richer intellectual well, one born of the profound transformation of both European and American architecture and a corollary, though less broad-based, movement in landscape architecture. Both had roots on both coasts.

Four of the key players in American residential garden design were Thomas J. Church, Garrett Eckbo, Dan Kiley, and James Rose. All four were educated at Harvard (Eckbo, Kiley, and Rose). Eckbo and Church were not only prolific, they were also proselytizers, traveling the country to promote the books they wrote, contributing to newspapers and magazines. Kiley and Rose were less voluble (for example, Rose's first book was published under a pseudonym) but no less influential in terms of the changes they made to residential landscape design. And these four were certainly not alone in transforming modern landscape architecture, but they were the outspoken theorists (and perhaps most adept at publicizing themselves) of a new, more holistic way of regarding the garden as an integral part of the house, an idea that became the essential tenet of the landscape theory that emerged in the middle twentieth century.

Eckbo, Kiley, and Rose met at Harvard in the late 1930s, where they hoped that the modernist fervor that had taken over at least part of the School of Architecture would also infiltrate the landscape program, though for the most part, it did not. The three of them co-authored a series of articles for *Architectural Record* expressing their new ideas about architecture. Church, born in 1902, predated the others, graduating from Harvard with a master's degree in landscape design and city planning in 1926. His education was classical—the thoroughgoing Beaux-Arts education that was the mainstay of the era would later be superseded, fueled by his travels—including meeting with the great Finnish architect Alvar Aalto—and by his burgeoning passion for modern art and architecture, all of which of course segued into landscape design.

GARRETT ECKBO was born in 1910, his mother American and his father Norwegian. His parents separated, and he moved with his mother to California, where they settled in Alameda. He enrolled in the landscape architecture program, then a full-fledged Beaux-Arts course of study, the University of California, Berkeley, at age nineteen, and in 1936 arrived at Harvard, where his lifelong philosophy began to emerge. He was tough, liberal-minded, and rebellious, especially against the proscriptions of traditional landscape architecture. He returned to California armed with new ideas, most of which—and more—he poured into his first book, *Landscape for Living,* published in 1950.

Landscape for Living was at once historical, theoretical, philosophical, polemical, and fervent, and it laid out the groundwork for much of what would be discussed in modern garden design for years to come. "Modern design is not another 'manner' to add to our bag of stylistic tricks; it is not a new kind of exterior decoration to be picked up my reading a couple of magazine articles of an evening or taking a short brush-up course during the dull summer season; it is not composed of ratchets, chevrons, zigs, zags, squirms, wiggles, or other juke-box tricks; it is not a new kind of doubletalk to be lifted from the shop-window designers jargon; it is not a matter of bending axes into spirals, or of rejuvenation nature with a new skirt-length or a new set of glands," he expounded. "Modern design is serious work."

For Eckbo, that serious work included rejecting preconceived academic notions (as he and his Harvard cohorts had) because they were stale and irrelevant. Eckbo's approach was at once embedded in the scientific process, relying on analysis and logic, but also on a far more abstract notion of creating space, he said. "One is with the objective of giving the richest, most plastic and satisfying form to the space which is being organized; the other is to concentrate always on that space as an arena, volume, background, and shelter for human life and activity."

Politically liberal and socially conscious, Eckbo had designed migrant worker camps for the Farm Security Administration when he was fresh from Harvard. Later, he found a like-minded partner in the Los Angeles architect Gregory Ain; together they designed progressive housing projects in several Los Angeles neighborhoods, including Planned Park Homes in Altadena, Avenel Cooperative House in Los Angeles's Silver Lake, and Mar Vista Tract in the Los Angeles neighborhood of the same name. His two firms—Eckbo, Royston and Williams and Eckbo, Dean, Austin, & Williams (which later became EDAW, renowned worldwide)—were among those that not only set the baseline of public and private landscape design in California, but also widely promulgated those ideas.

THOMAS CHURCH, eight years Eckbo's senior, graduated from Berkeley, and then went on to Harvard's graduate program in city planning and landscape architecture, graduating with an MFA in 1926. Early on, he fell under the influence of the compelling work being done in California by such architects as Bernard Maybeck in the Bay Area and farther south, in Pasadena primarily, Greene and Greene, but in the 1920s and early 1930s garden design had not progressed as far as architecture had; a trip to Europe in 1938 where he met Alvar Aalto, among others, and began to solidify his new thinking about landscape, rather seamlessly making the transition from designing formal, axial gardens to those in a more modern idiom that combined softer organic forms with strong geometric gestures. Professionally, Church was a mainstay of Northern California, but his clients were more geographically diverse—Texas, Michigan, and Mexico included.

His most famous and memorable work, the Donnell Pool and Garden at the southern edge of Sonoma, California, was done with the landscape architect Lawrence Halprin, then a member of his firm. It's a monument on its own—the first modern pool. It is fully preserved today, a simple but spectacular landscape on a spectacular site—a hillside plateau with a view (on a clear day) through Marin County to San Francisco. Its importance goes beyond the biomorphic bean shape; the pool and garden express ideas about adapting forms from nature rather than reshaping nature, which became a key tenet of modern landscape design.

Among Church's numerous innovations were to use hardier plants that needed less care from the harried modern homeowner and the addition of more "hardscape," including steps, fences, paving, seats, and curbs—as well as garden structures. Like Eckbo, he had a missionary's zeal about modern landscape design. His magazine writings arguably, made him the most famous landscape architect in the country. He wrote a column for the editor Elizabeth Gordon at *House Beautiful* through the duration of her twenty-year tenure, and that meant his name and his ideas were widely known across America.

His book, *Gardens Are for People*, came out in 1955, and though it was heavily oriented toward California, it was widely reviewed across the country in newspapers large and small, with no uncertain admiration. "No wonder Thomas D. Church is considered the leading landscape architect in the country today! For more than twenty years he has been in private practice and the articles he has prepared for magazines of the past eight years have brought his name to the attention of millions of people," wrote the *Tampa Tribune*. "You can enjoy outdoor living whether you have and 8-by-10 city back, a 50-by-100 suburban lot, or an acre or more in the country. The secret lies in the outdoor 'room' and *Gardens are for People* tells you how to make such rooms," wrote the Decatur, Illinois, *Herald*. "Thomas D. Church, the world's foremost landscape architect, believes in giving people what they want ... His gardens are highly individualized, each one suiting the way of life of the people who will live in it."

In 1967, a decade before Church retired, the *Los Angeles Times Home Magazine* published an eight-page story on his work that lent some perspective. "Thomas D. Church does not need more recognition," wrote Dan MacMasters. "The landscape architect from San Francisco has towered over his field for so long that fame has tended to obscure the details of his achievements. He is the victim of being of being taken for granted." MacMasters went on to point out that "the only garden that counts with him is the one that gets built. And it must be soundly built. He is a perfectionist in matters of drainage and masonry and carpentry, things an owner never notices until they go wrong. He has also analyzed the revolutionary changes that are reworking the American home landscape, so the he can solve the brand-new problems of a mechanized society that is grudging of time and space. Finally, he designs beautiful gardens."

The gardens of James Rose and Dan Kiley hold equal weight in the canon of landscape history, but they did not dominate the discussion or the local newspaper home design pages in the Northeast and Midwest, which is not to say they escaped notice altogether.

The enigmatic **JAMES ROSE** was the least well known of the four. The landscape architect and scholar Dean Cardasis, who runs the James Rose Center for Landscape Architectural Research and Design, described him as "elusive and difficult to get close to—and uncompromising, highly individual, and often contentious person whom one writer referred to as the 'James Dean of landscape architecture.' He drank too much and drove too fast, and argued too vehemently. Yet he made serene and contemplative gardens—'space sculptures,' he called them—and wrote not only sharp and penetrating criticism but also eloquent and even poetic descriptions of garden and landscape."

A high school dropout, Rose eventually enrolled at Cornell University then transferred to Harvard to study landscape design. At Harvard, he joined forces with Eckbo and Kiley, and the three co-authored a body of early work published in *Architectural Record* and *Pencil Points* (later to become *Progressive Architecture*). Rose's 1938 essay in *Pencil Points*, says in part: "Isn't is a little inconsistent, and perhaps unfair, to expect a Twentieth Century individual to step out of a stream-lined automobile and then flounder through a Rousseauian wilderness until he reaches a 'machine for living'? We cannot confine living, which is a process, to little segregated compartments that end at the edge of the nearest terrace where we are again asked to adjust ourselves to what, in its highest form, becomes an Eighteenth Century landscape painting."

His own home, built in 1953 on the Ho-Ho-Kus brook in Ridgewood, New Jersey, uses recycled materials and offers a window into his design ethos, fusing indoor and outdoor spaces. As Cardasis put it: "Rose's magnum opus provides us with an unusually comprehensive record of the mind of one of landscape architecture's most visionary modern thinkers and designers, as well as an alternative image of what America's suburbs could have been, and perhaps, still can be. In its rich expression of a small house and landscape as a single modern spatial unit, its integration with a mundane suburban site, and especially, its premeditated embrace of change, Rose's Ridgewood home was both a personal dream come true and a built critique of the American dream."

DANIEL URBAN KILEY—known widely as Dan—designed some of America's best-known and most important modernist landscapes, including those at the St. Louis Arch, Lincoln Center, the John F. Kennedy Library, the East Wing of the National Gallery of Art, and the Miller House and Garden in Columbus, Indiana. His work, which he termed "the poetry of space," was highly cerebral but also highly regarded. President Clinton honored him with the National Medal of the Arts in 1997, when he was eighty-four. Although he started his career in Washington, D.C., Kiley moved to Charlotte, Vermont, in 1950 and remained there until his death at the age of ninety-one in 2004. His fans included Prince Charles of England and the architect I.M. Pei.

The garden writer Anne Raver wrote eloquently about Kiley, describing him in one piece, "a link to history," adding that "for more than 60 years, his work has revealed an almost mystical sense of the land." Kiley himself spoke poetically—most of the time. He once said that "like a butterfly emerging from the chrysalis, I am always searching for the purest connection that holds us all together. Some form of sacred geometry. Sometimes the prevailing order is unseen, unknown." At other times, he was a contrarian, saying for example that the much-heralded and much analyzed allées of Moraine (or honey) locust trees leading to the Miller House, sometimes heralded as a turning point in the move to modernism in landscape design, were primarily a pragmatic gesture. "I planted those threes to shade the west side of the house. There needed to be an allée there, so why avoid it?"

Kiley designed the landscape for the Miller House in 1955. The house itself was designed by Eero Saarinen with interiors by Alexander Girard. The garden covers more than ten acres and uses hedges, bosques, meadows, pathways, and the much-admired allees to create, he said, "the sense of spaces folding and unfolding to join with one another. The result is that the landscape frame views in a way that it has as much, or more, impact as the architecture.

AN OBJECT IN THE LANDSCAPE

It goes without saying that the midcentury garden would not exist without the midcentury house. Without the latter, the former would not exist, and that is not either obvious or paradoxical. The brilliance and innovation of the garden, the radical change it brought was that, at its best, it made the house and garden part of one another.

By the mid-twentieth century, architecture moved away from the Beaux-Arts and more stylized notions of art deco into the streamlined moderne of the 1930s and '40s and the early modernism of the Bauhaus (and to a lesser extent, American architects), but for much of the western world the austere ideas of Le Corbusier of the "machine for living" dominated. By 1937 Walter Gropius had begun teaching architecture at Harvard, and others soon joined him, notably Marcel Breuer. Soon, Eckbo, Kiley, and Rose followed. They were hopeful that the progressive spirit that was taking over the study of architecture would also infuse new life and introduce new ideas into the architecture program, though such a fusion was not to happen.

Philosophically, modern American architecture (and this is true even today) falls into two camps that—at least in terms of the building of houses—can be separated by a simple preposition: *on* or *of*. The former, buildings *on* the land largely applied to the work that might best be considered Bauhaus-driven, led by such luminaries as Walter Gropius, Marcel Breuer, Mies van der Rohe, and Philip Johnson. The latter, architecture that is *of* the land, evolved more organically as a peculiarly American modernism, with its intellectual roots in Frank

Lloyd Wright's work and teaching; it reached its apex in Los Angeles where, at least in the years after World War II, modernism was practiced with a religious fervor. The best path to understanding this is by looking at period photographs; words do not always tell the truth, but images don't lie.

Historians report that at Harvard, Gropius showed little interest in landscape design, but that was not the case in the house he built for himself in Lincoln, Massachusetts, which was strongly connected to its garden. (The surmise is that this was driven by Gropius's second wife, Ise.) "A great deal of the charm of old houses is due to the mellowing effect of time and of their well-established gardens," wrote Walter Gropius in a 1949 essay for *House & Garden* about his house, which he'd constructed eleven years earlier after fleeing Nazi Germany and leaving his beloved Bauhaus behind to start a new life in America (where he was instrumental in bringing European modernism to the Western Hemisphere). "The appearance of our own house has changed within ten years because the landscaping and gardens have had time to grow up to our original plan. The house is opened up to take in a part of the surrounding area and extends beyond its enclosing walls; it reaches out with 'tentacles' of trellis, low walls, and planting design to delineate the outdoor living spaces and make them part of the overall composition. They provide a view of a natural stage on which the dramatic events of nature entertain us from morning to evening, summer and winter."

That same year, *House & Garden Magazine* featured several other modern houses, among them Philip Johnson's 1949 Glass House, about which the magazine said: "The protection provided by the trees was a determining factor in Philip C. Johnson's choice of glass; that, and the magnificent view over ridge after ridge of Connecticut hills." The Glass House, of course, is much more—the garden historian Magda Salvesen praises its witty use of architectural follies as "the most intriguing Twentieth Century riposte" to eighteenth-century landscape traditions. It was a dramatic moment for architecture and for modernism. "This huge rectangle of sheets of plate glass attracts so much attention from sightseers now that the New Canaan Police Force has to keep men on duty on weekends to keep traffic moving," according to a 1949 report in the *St. Louis Post-Dispatch*.

The Glass House was an object of awe, and it was not alone; throughout the Northeast and Midwest, especially, remarkable modern houses garnered both attention and admiration. Few, however, had landscapes. For many of America's most prominent modernists, houses had a foreground, the interior, and a background—the long view of the landscape—but the middle ground was seldom as important, comprising a lawn and perhaps specimen trees. Even Gropius's Bauhaus colleague Marcel Breuer, another émigré, favored natural materials, and many of his houses were built of stone and wood, but the love for those materials did not always extend into the garden.

FOREGROUND, MIDDLE, AND BACKGROUND

The most fertile ground for midcentury architecture was the West—particularly Southern California, where many architects were working with a different framework and architectural exploration and where innovation ruled. Southern California's dramatic settings offered fertile ground for a new architecture, starting with dramatic terrain that ranges from arid to rainy, warm to cool, and mountainous to coastal; the wide swath of the state from Santa Barbara to San Diego that includes Palm Springs and Palm Desert has beaches and deserts, hills and mountains, and sites that run the gamut from simple to precarious. Frank Lloyd Wright and later his son Lloyd made a mark there, but by the 1930s it was two European immigrants—Rudolph Schindler and Richard Neutra—who dominated the architectural thinking.

Neutra's work provides the most compelling insight and had the most pervasive impact on landscape design. "I try to make a house like a flowerpot in which you can root something and out of which family life will bloom. It's not so much a question of ornamenting the flowerpot as of fabricating it in such a way that something healthy and beautiful can grow in and out of it," he once said. For Neutra, architecture involved what he called "biological realism," and that meant re-centering the idea of what architecture is about, using it to reunite man and nature. Writing of Neutra in 1977, nine years after the architect's death and on the occasion of his posthumous Gold Medal from the American Institute of Architects, the critic John Dreyfuss said of him:

"To achieve that complex harmony, Neutra resorted to simplicity: crisp, cubistic residences emphasizing horizontal lines. They were built of steel, stucco and glass and, in later years, wood and stone as well. But it was glass upon which Neutra most relied to define his spaces without confining them. His pioneering use of great planes of glass brought the outs in and let the inside out to the point that in Neutra houses there can be uncertainty about whether one is indoors or outdoors. Neutra structures foster meaningful relationships between their residents and nature, which was one of the architect's intentions."

That quality is what distinguishes Neutra from his East Coast (and many of his West Coast) counterparts. While Philip Johnson, for example, created a house in a clearing surrounded by the woods beyond, really a foreground and a background, Neutra consciously worked to create a foreground, middle ground, and background. The great photographer Julius Shulman took his first-ever architectural photograph of Neutra's Kun House 2, and it informed his photography to follow and really—because we see so much of what we know of our built environment through the lens of a camera—our understanding of midcentury architecture landscape design.

Neutra was ferocious in expressing his beliefs, imparting his ideas in such books as *Survival Through Design*, published in 1954, and *Life and Human Habitat*, published in 1956 and released in English, Italian, German, and Spanish. Both books were featured as cover stories complete with drawings (for one) and photos of the architect and his work in the widely read *Saturday Review*, the former positively and the latter not so much. The positive review came from Douglas Haskell, at the time the editor of *Architectural Forum* in *House and Home* magazine, who wrote, "Look in any encyclopedia or history of art and you will find a definition of architecture as some kind or another of the fine building. Look in Neutra and you will see that the conscious arrangement or rearrangement of any human surrounds creates a healthful and joyous impact on human nerves. In one fine phrase Neutra calls the architect dealing with environment a 'gardener of nervous growth.'"The careffiul and subtle layering of Neutra's design and his fastidious attention to both the intimate and grander connections of a house to its natural setting become apparent in Shulman's remarkable body of photographic work, providing a clear window into if not the architect's intentions, his achievements. This is not to discount the contributions of other Los Angeles architects—the fast-growing "Southland" abounded with designers and builders in that era. Among the many were Pierre Koenig, Craig Ellwood, Raphael Soriano, A. Quincy Jones, Edward Fickett, John Lautner, Thornton Abell, Charles and Ray Eames, as well as the under-sung Greta Magnusson-Grossman and the short-lived Gordon Drake; and in Palm Springs, there was William Krisel, Albert Frey, and William F. Cody (and this is by no means a complete list). Many of these architects left an important legacy of beautiful houses with fine outdoor spaces that are still cherished today.

ORGANIC MODERNISM

The American Midwest, of course, had produced Frank Lloyd Wright and his far more organic architecture, truly rooted in the land. There is no more powerful example of this than Fallingwater, where land and building join in a single unified—and dramatic—composition. In the years after World War II, Wright developed his Usonian house idea of smaller and more affordable houses that often also connected closely with the landscape; spanning the decades before and after World War II, Usonian houses were built both individually—such as the Zimmerman House in Manchester, New Hampshire, which is now under the ownership of the Aldrich Museum—or in clusters, as is the case with the Usonia District in New York's Westchester County.

Wright's followers notably included Alfred Browning Parker in Miami, who practiced an almost macrobiotic form of modernism, one in which nature and architecture were often so unified that his early houses had no windows or screens but rather "persiana" shutters that opened to the tropical breezes. Parker's houses, like Wright's, imparted a fully idealized idea of architecture, and in the case of Miami, of a romantic relationship between man and nature, architecture and landscape. "His buildings were pavilions in nature," said the architect and scholar Allan Shulman.

In Florida, the land and climate were entirely different from almost anywhere else in the country and warm year-round—not only enticing thousands of returning GIs to become sun seekers but also attracting a new generation of architects who saw the flat, sandy, coastal landscape as a blank slate for experimentation. In Sarasota, Paul Rudolph explored ways to make a house sit as lightly as possible on the land as well as ways to filter sun and create shade. He, along with the architects who joined him there, left an inimitable legacy. In Miami, the Russian-born Igor Polevitzky was perhaps the most ambitiously experimental of the city's modernists. He created a prototype "birdcage" house that was essentially a screened pavilion, thus layering the landscape and providing a sequence leading from inside out or outside in.

LITTLE BOXES, NOT ALL DRESSED IN TICKY TACKY...

The true social and cultural impact came in a different way, in housing for the masses—the "little boxes" celebrated and excoriated in literature, film, television, sociology, and perhaps most memorably, song. They came in many shapes, sizes, and colors, these little boxes. It was efficient, straightforward in design and construction, and easy to replicate; thirteen million new houses were built in the two decades after World War II.

The Cape Cod house—with its sloping roof and often, dormers—came first, but it was soon supplanted by the ranch house and then the split-level; for the most part those earliest houses were simple structures, neither architectural nor especially imaginative. It was definitely not "high style" modernism, as the scholar Barbara Miller Lane points out in her landmark study of postwar housing. She notes that while the architecture and design magazines were paying attention to and lauding praises on the brilliant work of American modernists, most Americans sought something simpler as the forms of modernism "seemed foolish or alien. The great majority of Americans saw the split-level or the ranch as the true 'modern' house." The art historian Gwendolyn Wright noted that most intellectuals have tried to ignore suburbia, at least the mass-produced postwar suburbia "as if were an embarrassing cultural fluke."

The split-level is an Eastern invention, attributed to the Long Island architect Herman York, who designed for the Levitts in the 1940s. The ranch house has much deeper roots in the American West, in the low-slung Spanish-style houses that date back to the nineteenth century. In the twentieth century, the softer edges (heavy stucco, barrel tile) of the Spanish ranch house gave way to a more modern style, but key factors remained—long, low-slung, hipped rooflines being a key—along with more up-to-date innovations such as attached garages and open floor plans.

Most of this can be attributed to the brilliant and colorful Cliff May, whose family roots were in the rugged ranching tradition of South California. May introduced the ranch house—or rather reintroduced it—in the 1930s and then went on to hone his craft in the postwar years.

California was the postwar Promised Land, offering a desirable climate and jobs, and more—the promise of easy living, indoor/outdoor a must. Into this equation came the builders whose new suburban housing developments offered exactly that, easy living and, in so doing, became symbols of a time and a place. Among them is the Alexander Construction Company, whose Palm Springs subdivisions were designed by William Krisel and Dan Palmer, and the prolific Joseph Eichler, whose tract houses encircled the San Francisco Bay area and many points south. Eichler was not just a developer but also a missionary who believed that good architecture should be available to the masses and who called upon some of California's best modern designers. Eichler's houses were one story, revolved around an atrium, and offered open floor plans for modern living.

Eichler held what one might call a commercial idealism—he was politically liberal and his ideas were progressive. He also was productive, ultimately building some 13,000 homes. Elsewhere, the optimism and progressive spirit of the postwar era produced other kinds of idealized communities, including Arapahoe Acres outside of Denver and Hollin Hills in Virginia, which was designed by the Washington, D.C. architect Charles Goodman and had a landscape plan from Dan Kiley. The era was one marked by an energetic sense of exploration—in this case of new technologies—that produced such early experiments in prefabricated houses as Lustron and Leisurama, further increasing the pace of new construction.

INDUSTRIAL REVOLUTION

A major premise of midcentury design—whether high art or mass production—was that the garden was an extension to the home, not an accessory. In warmer climates, this meant year-round outdoor living replete with patios and pools. Family life moved outside. The new modern home gave rise, too, to an array of new industries and burgeoning product offerings—pools, patio pavers, planters, awnings, and most of all, furniture. "Today's landscape is not complete without structural forms—a roof for shades, screens for privacy, permanent seating facilities and planters for accent," wrote the *Los Angeles Times* in April 1955. Indeed, the home and garden sections of newspapers and magazines were filled with advice and encouragement.

In July 1955, Phoenix's *Arizona Republic* newspaper summarized it this way: "Not too many years ago, there was a small, specialized group of 'summer furniture.' Its use was limited to a few months on the porch or in the back yard. Designs were not particularly smart, often not even comfortable, but they provided outdoor seating. Today 'summer furniture' offers many of the smartest designs from the drawing boards of talented artists. And 'summer' is a misnomer, because these attractive pieces a found a place indoors throughout the years."

The introduction of comparatively new materials—plastics and Fiberglas among them—propelled industry, as did the many new uses discovered for existing materials. The country was freed from the shortages of wartime, when raw materials were diverted for military use. Aluminum, which was invented in the early nineteenth century, became highly popularized after World War I, primarily because it was less expensive than other materials and lightweight but strong, making it ideal for outdoor use in both awnings and furniture. The ubiquitous aluminum folding chair came into popularity starting in 1947, when it was fabricated in Brooklyn; other manufacturers were soon to follow, and by the mid-1950s an assortment of chairs sported bright-hued plastic webbing and were sold in garden stores, furniture stores, and even grocery stores. A typical price was $3.95.

That same year, Edgar Bartolucci and John J. Waldheim designed the Barwa chair, a rocking lounger that riffed on the bentwood work of the Austrian firm Thonet (as well as prewar modern offerings from Le Corbusier and Mies van der Rohe). The Barwa was made of aluminum tubing with a stretched canvas seat. "Enjoy Outdoor Living at Home," proclaimed one advertisement. "You'll feel wonderful relaxing in the Aluminum Barwa Chair."

Another ubiquitous outdoor chair with lofty design roots and greater longevity was the butterfly chair, invented in Argentina by Antonio Bonet, Juan Kurchan, and Jorge Ferrari-Hardoy in 1938; it quickly caught the eye of Edgar Kauffman Jr., at the time a curator at the Museum of Modern Art and another for his parents' very famous home, Fallingwater. Knoll acquired the rights in 1947, but the company failed to acquire a patent and by 1951 the butterfly chair went into wide production and distribution, selling at times for as little as $8.95.

The design and fabrication of outdoor furniture is closely tied to the course of history—for example the Hawaiian designer Walter Lamb created a line of bronze outdoor furniture from piping pulled out of the water at Pearl Harbor. In the early twentieth century, designers had begun experimenting with the use of metals in furniture and construction (witness the work that came from the Bauhaus). But World War II meant the diverting of resources to military production, so that it was not until the later 1940s that the materials that would form the basis of so much outdoor furniture became widely available again.

In these postwar years, the outdoor furniture industry came to full life with such long-lasting and sought-after lines as Woodard's Sculptura, Clark's Ames Aire, and Homecrest's Bottemiller. Leading designers of the day—including Americans Harry Bertoia, Charles Eames, Raymond Loewy, and the Italian architect Maurizio Tempestini—produced furniture for the patio and garden. The New York–based John B. Salterini Inc., with Tempestini as the chief designer, produced a wide line of wrought iron furniture that attracted wide national attention at home shows and in newspapers countrywide. The syndicated writer Amy Rollinson reported from the Grand Rapids summer furniture market in June 1951 that "Maurizio Tempestini is a gentleman from Florence who specializes in design the homes of wealthier Romans and at the same time mass-producing high style wrought iron furniture for Americans of above-average taste and average pocketbooks. Next to the Scandinavian influence it is the Tempestini 'tempest' which is causing news at the show here . . ."

Likewise, the furniture of the California-based firm of Van Keppel-Green generated its own share of press. A 1953 story in the *Arizona Republic* announced that "Van Keppel-Green designs rarely date or become obsolescent. They usually become classics . . ." The designer Richard Schultz joined Knoll in 1953 and designed his classic petal table soon thereafter. However, it was in the mid-1960s, when he was commissioned by Florence Knoll Bassett, who had by then moved to Miami, to design a suite of poolside furniture (known as the 1966 line) that became an instant classic. "Indoors or out, these graceful contemporary pieces make light of sitting in 'floating' mesh slings," wrote Grace Madley in the *Philadelphia Inquirer*.

The attention was warranted. In 1951, the American furniture industry earned $200 million dollars—which was the equivalent of more than $1 billion in 2020.

DO-IT-YOURSELF

The move to the suburbs, whether it was to a ranch or split-level or a modified Cape Cod, meant a paradigm shift not just in how we built houses but also in how we lived in them and with them. The shift was not just in authorship but in ownership. As America moved to to compact new houses in burgeoning subdivisions, a new kind of garden design emerged: a do-it-yourself art.

In 1956, Garrett Eckbo published a "bible" for homeowners, *The Art of Home Landscaping*. "The purpose of this book is to help you solve the typical average, common home-planning problems that appear in the outdoors around all our houses," reads the first sentence of the first chapter, entitled "Why Landscape?" Eckbo launches the book with a parable about two fictional suburban couples, the first of whom (the Newfields) does a random and haphazard job on landscaping their new home while the second couple (Henry and Martha Overbee) draws grids and measures and studies the lot to figure out optimal spots for planting. "To shorten a long story," wrote Eckbo, "the Overbees spent several weekends working out a plan. Four rolls of cheap tracing paper and two dozen pencils later they arrived at a scheme which seemed to solve their problems." The parable went on to point out that the Newfields were wondering why their new neighbors were spending so much time fussing over something so simple, but the Overbees persisted: "They made endless little diagrams of the right sizes, shapes and descriptions for these various elements, and they made endless patterns for dividing their yard space up in such a way as to fit in all these elements and make them work."

Weeks passed, and the Overbees were still planning and preparing, regarding the lot and extending the porch while the neighbors, said Eckbo, "relaxed into friendly sidewalk superintendence, and there were numerous good-natured debates over whys, wherefores, and hows." Of course, we all know where this story is headed: the Newfields had put all the plants in the wrong place and the grass left them with a big mowing burden, plus the terrace was inadequate, and more. But the Overbees' new landscape was a triumph—and an inspiration.

This may seem quaint, almost whimsical, but the truth was there. Houses were being constructed at a fierce rate, and for the most part, they came with a yard and grass, maybe some trees or a bush or two, but they were not landscaped in any sense of the word. Though it varied from place to place and region to region, these yards were generally small and houses close together.

In turn, this gave rise to not so much an industry but a movement—the do-it-yourself landscape. Newspapers from coast to coast featured garden stories telling homeowners "Your Garden Can Be An Open Room" or exhorting readers of the *Los Angeles Times* that "Gardens are an extension of the indoors and can be another enjoyable room for living when designed to take into consideration the hobbies, children, and animals of the family."

"Well what do we mean by 'modern design?" asked Eckbo in another *Los Angeles Times* piece from 1952. Eckbo and Church were both often featured in the pages of newspapers—most frequently in California, but also across the country. "Do we mean flat roofs, glass walls, no decoration, no partitions inside and more outside, strange curves, angles, forms and colors; materials used in unexpected ways, abstractions, climate control, glass blocks, concrete, gardens with tropical foliage? We may mean all of these, but we don't necessarily mean any of them. For fundamentally the serious designer called 'modern' is in search of the be possible solution to a given problem."

Newspapers became a forum for modern garden designers to preach their gospel. Edward Huntsman Trout, another of Los Angeles's postwar landscape architects, published a spirited defense of the unadorned wall in April 1952. Eckbo's partner Frances H. Dean (the firm was Eckbo, Dean, Austin, and Williams, EDAW) wrote in that same edition of the *Los Angeles Times* urging homeowners and homebuilders to consider the house and the garden as one, saying: "The gardens should be a continuous development in every respect with the house as a central element composed of a good selection of plants in a well-organized arrangement. However, consider the house as the center from which all things revolve, the possibilities of extending the fabric and materials into the garden are endless. The greater the gamut of materials, natural and processed, the greater the possibilities of produce a great variety of gardens, natural to refined."

A great proponent of the designed garden was Shan Stewart, whose garden advice appeared in the *Los Angeles Times* during the 1950s and 1960s and who contributed such articles as "Rock Texture . . . and How to Get It." His "Lightweight, for Leisure Hours" (this about rattan furniture) began, "Fashion does not require patio furniture to be of one styling or made of the same material, but with the wide selection on the market today—wrought iron, tubular brass, steel , aluminum, wood, reed, cane, canvas and plastic—one could easily end up with a hodgepodge."

Stewart's heavily illustrated step-by-step book entitled *Planning and Building Your Patio*, published in 1954, opens by pointing out that, "Actually building the right kind of patio is very simple, and it requires only a little effort and expense. It's a place for your children to play away from the street; it's a clean, dry place for all season of the year; it saves wear and tear on your house; it provides for your leisure, reduces your maintenance costs and minimizes the never-ending grass cutting. Above all, it increases your property value by many times its cost . . ." Stewart also added that "patio building can be so much fun," an important mantra for this new way of living.

The bible, of course, was Garrett Eckbo's *The Art of Home Landscaping*, but there were also numerous other books of advice, plans, drawings, and photos. Some were regional; those for the Northeast and Pacific Northwest, Midwest, for Florida or Hawaii and other tropical climates focused largely on plants and trees. *The Modern Family Garden Book* by Roy E. Biles, published first in 1935 and then reissued in 1940 and 1941, offered a step-by-step guide to planting, complete with inspirational quotes from an array of poets and detailed drawings to guide the novice gardener.

By the 1960s, the offerings were even more substantial. Alice Recknagel Ireys, a graduate of the Cambridge School of Architecture and Landscape Architecture for Women (then affiliated with Smith College and in 1942 absorbed by Harvard), produced *How to Plan and Plant Your Own Property* in 1967, a thoroughgoing volume that offered detailed working plans. Alice Upham Smith, a landscape architect from Mountain Home, Arkansas, and herself a graduate of the Cambridge School published *Patios, Terraces, Decks, and Roof Gardens* in 1969; it likewise contained drawings along with the photography. In introducing her book, Smith pointed out that "as we have more leisure the patio or terrace becomes almost essential to the enjoyment of life in the garden and an important element of landscape design. In many cases it is almost an extension of the house, adding space for the casual entertaining we all enjoy so much." Smith went on to point out the importance of planning, of creating a "pleasing picture" though the changing seasons and then listed some of the considerations: "fixtures for garden lighting, sprays and electronic insect-killers, gas and electric barbecues, and outdoor fireplaces for cool evenings."

The very thorough *Practical Guide to Home Landscaping*, published by *Reader's Digest*, featured charts, diagrams, drawings, and photos and drew on the expertise of a number of the country's most prominent landscape architects, including Thomas Church, Theodore Osmundson, Douglas Baylis, and Donald H. Parker—part of a much longer list of participants. Along with *Reader's Digest*, a host of magazines—from *Popular Mechanics* at the practical end to *Time* and *Life* to *House & Garden* at the high end—published garden books, whether as practical guides or lofty inspiration. Much of this was reiterated in the material that appeared on their periodical pages, where countless articles offered homeowners attainable dreams, often with specifics including schematics, planting plans, instructions, and buying guides.

House Beautiful was a great proponent of the modern garden. Its editor through the midcentury, Elizabeth Gordon, was an ardent supporter of Frank Lloyd Wright and his followers; she was also a fervent foe of Bauhaus-propelled design, which she saw as a threat to her idea of the American way of life first ("no children, no dogs, extremely meager kitchen facilities") and impractical because in such houses, she said, you overheated in summer and froze in winter. In *House Beautiful*, Gordon had a pulpit, and she used it to not only publish Thomas Church's monthly columns but also to endorse a more organic approach to modern work, including that of Cliff May, A. Quincy Jones, William Wurster, Joseph Esherick, Hamilton Harwell Harris, and of course, Alfred Browning Parker.

However, the most influential postwar publisher/proselytizer/promulgator of hands-on home and garden design, particularly in the West and Southwest, was *Sunset Magazine*. *Sunset* produced numerous books offering ideas for landscaping and garden plans in general as well as specialized guides for patios, structures, art in the garden, and more. Though the magazine's demographics were quite specifically focused on homeowners in the West, the books found wide readership across the country.

Many of the *Sunset* books were updated and reissued every few years, keeping them current. The books were amply illustrated with diagrams, plans, and photographs that, though black and white, amply showed the promised lushness of the homeowner's new landscape. The photos often also held out the promise of a better life—dad barbecuing, kids playing, mom sunbathing—that only underscored all the practical and motivational advice within. The 1965 third printing of *Garden Plans* was filled with advice in chapters with such titles as "Bricks Are Basis, Plants Are Pleasure" or "A Long Lot Can Look Wide." The garden plans shown in *Garden Plans* were similarly inspiring, among them: "A Refuge for Contemplation," or "More Privacy, Less Upkeep," or "Light By Day, Bright By Night." Still others offered direct advice and instructions for making planters, sheds, greenhouses, decks, walls, steps, trellises, pergolas, and more.

The books tell a fairly complete story of the era in and of themselves, documenting outdoor spaces for the desert and woodlands, for the beach and for lakefronts and the river's edge. Sunset published guides for "Western" living as well as a guide to building Japanese gardens, a trend that had begun under the influence of Frank Lloyd Wright and was further promulgated by Elizabeth Gordon and *House Beautiful* but brought home, to the masses, by *Sunset*.

And home it came, accepted first perhaps reluctantly and then embraced. Writing in *America's Garden Book* (1939), one of the popular handbooks of its time, the landscape architect James Bush-Brown and his wife, the horticulturalist Louise Bush-Brown, devoted just four paragraphs to a somewhat mixed appraisal of "contemporary design"—in a book of 754 pages. The Bush-Browns found in general that modern landscape design relied too much on materials and too little on plants, arguing that "landscape design is a method of making compositions which achieve harmony and balance without symmetry," noting that contemporary landscape design show "no evident similarity to established styles, and even not much expectation of evolving a new style."

It's clear, however, that they were not as sure of their opinions as their original premise might imply, and to hedge their bets, they added:

"Modern design has various expressions. It cannot be limited within an accurate definition. It is buoyant, surprising, joyous, original, and ever evolving new forms by experiment. At its best it recognizes the demands, limitations and opportunities of the site. It captures something of the mood of the environs. It contributes something fresh to the art of living, and it makes appreciative use of the beauty of created and natural forms."

Time (as the cliché goes) would tell, and time proved them wrong.

MODERN MASTERWORKS

REIMAGINING THE MIDCENTURY HOUSE AND GARDEN

In 1953, the architect-turned-sculptor Tony Smith designed a house for the collector Fred Olson and his wife, Florence, on a rocky hilltop in Guilford, Connecticut. Decades later, it went up for sale, and the prospective buyer announced his intention to demolish it. That never happened. The Olsons' daughter, Elizabeth Kyburg, discovered the neighborhood's governing bylaws allowed the seller to reject a buyer and quite dramatically snatched the house from the sure jaws of death. Instead, the cinematographer Jeff Preiss and his wife, the painter Rebecca Quaytman, bought it and in turn brought the house and its rugged naturalistic setting back to a near-original state under the guidance of the New York architect John Keenen. And Keenen, with the assistance and advice of the landscape architect Edwina von Gal, further restored the house's rather wild and rustic landscape.

Not every important midcentury house has such a Cinderella story to tell, however. Notoriously, Richard Neutra's 1963 Maslon house in Rancho Mirage, California, was destroyed sight unseen by its new owner. John Lautner's 1951 Shusett House in Beverly Hills was torn down in 2010. Bought at auction in 2016 and widely considered a masterpiece, O'Neil Ford's Penson House in Dallas lasted mere months before its new owner demolished it. More recently, the Ellwood Zimmerman House in Los

Angeles, designed by Craig Ellwood in 1950, was razed after its lot sold for a figure in the double-digit millions, destined to be replaced with a "modern farmhouse," and Alfred Browning Parker's 1963 Sea Aerie in Coral Gables, Florida, fell prey to a legal loophole allowing demolition of single-family homes in flood-prone areas.

To be sure, the midcentury house has long faced a precarious future. Tastes change. Lifestyles change. The small "convenience" kitchen of the 1950s is not the vast cook's kitchen of today. There was a yard to play in, not a media room. Children sometimes shared a bedroom. Flat roofs leak. Climates change. Rivers rise. Seas rise. The houses were often experimental, using new materials that didn't necessarily hold up over the decades. With the rise of air-conditioning, the airy appeal of a house that opened wide to the outdoors held less appeal. Video games replaced outdoor play, and along the way, the barbeque on the patio lost its luster.

That's the bad news, and to be sure, there's plenty of it. But in the last two decades, awareness of our fragile and often-jeopardized modernist heritage has grown and lifestyles have changed once again. Today a new generation yearns for simplicity, though not necessarily out of nostalgia, and the indoor-outdoor life promised by the midcentury house has a new and ever-growing appeal to new homeowners.

OLD QUARRY

TONY SMITH, PELLI ARCHITECTS / REED HILDERBRAND

GUILFORD, CONNECTICUT

Formerly forgotten but never in jeopardy, this Tony Smith house features a new landscape that poetically expands the meaning of site-specific design

OPPOSITE A mass planting of ferns fills in some of the vertical space between the ground and the house, which is raised on pilotis, without interrupting the house's sculptural clarity. A rough-hewn path inspired by the site's historic quarry leads the way to the actual entry stair.

The architect (later turned sculptor) Tony Smith's second venture on the land in Guilford, Connecticut, known as Old Quarry, was just down the hill from the first house he designed. Both were part of a subdivision redevelopment in a former waterfront quarry where many of the homeowners have obscured the rugged coastal beauty of the site under a sweep of suburban lawn.

More than fifty years after it was built, the quickly deteriorating house was purchased by the architect Rafael Pelli, who restored the house and selected the prominent landscape architecture firm of Reed Hilderbrand to create a setting that fit the site. The design needed to be durable, easy to care for, and walkable and at the same time honor Smith's architecture. In turn Reed Hilderbrand sought to celebrate the "found condition" of the historic quarry that had given way to housing and make the most of the dramatic coastal setting.

The house sits on a small slice of craggy broken rock between Long Island Sound and a granite escarpment leading to higher ground. Using the site's own granite—quarry refuse and bedrock—the designers reordered and manipulated the land to, as they termed it, "heighten the experience of the found conditions and to integrate the building volumes with the site's larger patterns."

The house itself was set on steel columns, an expression of the idea that the quarry, which the designers termed "part ruin, part natural system," was to be observed rather than occupied. Reed Hilderbrand sought to celebrate this, noting that it took "careful stewardship and light-handed reworking of the site stone" to do so. The landscape architects turned quarry tailings into pathways, the better to see the rough-hewn landscape and enhancing the experience. The goal was to create a landscape that seemed geological, almost archeological, as if it had been unearthed.

It was an iterative process. An addition to the house was inserted among the trees. Reed Hilderbrand reused refuse stone wherever possible, planted new trees where they could,

restored woodlands, and replanted with new and diverse trees where existing trees (most of them Norway maples) were removed. This was not an instant fix; the landscape architects worked on Old Quarry for several years, applying hand weeding and organic maintenance practices to rid the land of invasive exotic plants and trees and, as the designers termed it, allowing "a seedbed of scrappy natives" to grow. To preserve the views, there are herbaceous and woody plants that remain low to the ground—ferns, bearberry, lowbush blueberry. Said the landscape architects: "Our work creates occupiable ground for walking and exploring, and a context strong enough to respond to the sculptural clarity of the building."

RIGHT Salvaged granite is stacked in a sculptural "vein" that leads from the house to the remnant borrow pit.

OPPOSITE The house's site rests on a rocky escarpment to the side of Long Island Sound; the restored landscape, long buried under ivy and other invasive nonnative plants, celebrates the quarry's history and is designed to be low impact to maintain the health of the body of water.

LEFT The house's private rooms are carefully enclosed in a renewed band of woodland for privacy and separation from the adjacent addition.

OPPOSITE Years of careful invasive removal results in a landscape that can now host ferns, bearberry, lowbush blueberry, and climate-adapted trees.

SILVERTOP

JOHN LAUTNER, BARBARA BESTOR / GARRETT ECKBO, MIA LEHRER

LOS ANGELES, CALIFORNIA

A fastidious and fearless restoration preserves this aerodynamic, avant-garde Los Angeles landmark

OPPOSITE Silvertop's famous architecture that seems to make the house levitate on the hill is emphasized by parallel curves on the patio and the planting area filled with zoysia grass as ground cover below. The crow's nest offers even more panoramic views.

In 1959, the long-gone *Hollywood Evening Citizen News* reported on an "unusual home" then under construction in Silver Lake, quoting the architect, John Lautner, this way: "There must be a main idea in architectural design, and with me it is to give individual joy or freedom—a pleasure, an emotion that comes to a person through a creation that especially suits him."

Of the many excellent and intriguing architects at work in Los Angeles, and indeed much of California, in the postwar era, Lautner stood out for his architectural derring-do, his design ambition, and his almost space-age sensibilities, even a decade or so before there was what we could truly call a space age. The article pointed out that he was in many ways the heir to and protégé of Frank Lloyd Wright, and indeed, his work—so manifestly evident in the house called Silvertop—is at once organic and aerodynamic.

It was built for a businessman/inventor named Kenneth Reiner, whose own futuristic vision may even have exceeded Lautner's. But destiny intervened; Reiner's business failed before the house was fully completed, and he never moved into it. Instead, it sat empty until it was purchased in a bankruptcy sale by a couple who went on to live there for forty years. In 2014, music executive Luke Wood purchased it and hired the architect Barbara Bestor, not just to renovate it but to fulfill its original intent. Bestor not only did assiduous research but hired a dream team of associates, including the landscape architect Mia Lehrer of Studio-MLA.

In 2018 the veteran Los Angeles architecture writer Michael Webb took an in-depth look at the restored Silvertop, a house he had once toured with Lautner himself. "Drama is the hallmark of Silvertop," he said. In his eloquent and admiring article for *DesignLA Magazine*, Webb described the landscape as he saw it, looking out from the living room where floor-to-ceiling glazing "frames a panorama of the city to the east, while the westerly view to the Hollywood Hills is shaded by two tall trees. An aged sycamore serves as a site-specific sculpture, and another tree penetrates a hole in the projecting roof plane." Tall saguaro cacti hug yet another floor-to-ceiling glass wall as if they are sculptural objects. Lehrer designed the garden to extend to the edge of the site, again reinforcing the illusion of Silvertop as a sculpture suspended in space.

LEFT The point of arrival at the top of the steep drive is announced by a planter box filled with climate-adapted plants that benefit from the skylight above.

OPPOSITE Period-appropriate chairs continue the elliptical theme while a mature sycamore, bromeliads, and palms direct views out over the city.

RIGHT Plantings on the far side of the elliptical infinity pool—often described as the first infinity pool—are kept low so as not to obstruct city views, but do include pops of colorful blooms to draw the eye.

OPPOSITE, LEFT Columnar euphorbias of exactly the right height are tucked under the broad eaves just outside Lautner's famous fully retractable glass wall.

OPPOSITE, RIGHT Floor-to-ceiling glass windows reveal how effectively the outside plantings screen the house from the neighbors, allow views of low shrubs from the interior, and even incorporate an indoor terrarium.

RIGHT Silver boulders and a silver-trunked sycamore create a natural sculpture garden.

OPPOSITE The restored back patio also uses ellipses at the ground plane, in the form of shaped planting beds and sidewalks, and retains the cut-out slot that still accommodates a large fir tree.

THE FROST HOUSE

EMIL TESSIN / GROUNDWORK DESIGN

MICHIGAN CITY, INDIANA

A prefab house that pays homage to both Eames and Mondrian is brought back to life with a careful and erudite restoration and a landscape to match

OPPOSITE Trees original to the three-quarter-acre site are limbed up to allow full views to the Mondrian-esque prefab house's colorful panels. Below this, "wave berms" of groundcover allow the rectilinear geometry of the architecture to "dissolve" into more naturalistic lines.

The recent owners of the Frost House, Karen Valentine and Robert Coscarelli, term themselves "stewards" of this immaculate, almost untouched experimental modern house in Michigan City, Indiana. They bought it in 2016, and before that it had been in the hands of a single family since 1964, when the house was completed. The house has the geometric sensibilities and primary colors of the famous Eames House or a Piet Mondrian painting. It also has a back story: it is an aluminum prefab built as a sales model to show off the patented system invented by the now-long-since-defunct Alside Homes Company (an early side business of the still-functioning siding company, Alside, Inc.) of Akron, Ohio, and designed by Emil Tessin. Tessin, the company's in-house architect, created twenty-two different configurations for a planned two hundred prefab houses. This house had belonged to Dr. Robert Frost, a forensic pathologist, and his wife, Amelia. But there was more: the interiors include two amazing glass partitions designed by Paul McCobb, and it was filled with original Knoll furniture.

Though the house was an almost mummified time capsule, the garden in the three-quarter-acre lot that the long Alside homes require was not. To that end, Valentine and Coscarelli hired Chicago landscape architect Julie deLeon of Groundwork Design to add a swimming pool (this is a weekend getaway, after all) and create a landscape befitting the midcentury legacy of the house. "I wanted to pay tremendous homage to the architecture," says deLeon.

The property had some massive established trees but otherwise was overgrown with shrubbery—except in the side lot, which was bare. The key element was the addition of a "glass" (actually translucent Plexiglas) wall that echoes the McCobb partitions inside and offers privacy from the neighbors. The wall had existed in the original yard only as a fragment on one side of the property, but she extended it from front to back to become not just a defining feature of the landscape but also an artistic element within it. The goal, she says, was to make it seem like it had been there a long time.

DeLeon decided that instead of simply ripping out the longstanding shrubs (mostly juniper) she would try to save them. She created "wave berms" alongside the long, narrow pool bordered by concrete; from the pool, the view is of the neighboring forest preserve, which in turn she says, "makes you feel buried under the oaks and elms and ash trees."

Another addition was a patio in the back, a design that evolved after Valentine, Coscarelli, and deLeon had pored over as many images of Alside prefab homes as they could find. The boulders were a nod to midcentury gardens on rocky terrain across the county.

Although the "found condition" of the landscape was far more prone to curves and berms, deLeon sought to have the planting beds be structural and geometric, particularly around the new pool, in keeping with the rigorous mathematical composition of the house. "I wanted to honor the rectilinear lines of the house," she says. She did however let part of the geometry dissolve, at one point, into a more naturalistic and soft-edged vignette at the front of the property. The plant material includes perennials, ornamentals, and dogwood, along with the juniper hedges and another hedge of yews that lines the back of the property, which are evergreen and thus offer some color in the white of winter.

Only a dozen of the Alside aluminum houses that Tessin designed are known to be standing. The company had big ambitions for their idea, but it was not one that caught on with its Midwestern constituency. The project was abandoned, and Tessier moved on, but Robert and Amelia Frost stayed true to their piece of the modern dream. It's encouraging to see it now expanded and enhanced.

LEFT, ABOVE A garden room with period-appropriate furniture allows enjoyment of the garden even in Indiana winters, when careful use of evergreens provides interest against the snow.

LEFT, BELOW Part of the yard in frequent shade thanks to the tall established trees is reserved for quiet contemplation in classic midcentury butterfly chairs and dog exercise.

OPPOSITE The boulder next to this patio is in homage to midcentury homes first designed in warmer parts of the country.

LEFT The Fiberglas fence is intended to echo the materials of the original midcentury partitions inside the house, provide privacy from neighbors, as well as allow partial views out and up to the woodland beyond.

OPPOSITE A pool area is screened from neighbors thanks to *Cornus kousa*, *Thuja occidentalis* 'Wintergreen', and *Hydrangea paniculata* 'Limelight'. The beds along the far sides provide additional textural interest thanks to, at left, *Sesleria autumnalis*, *Allium* 'Summer Beauty', *Stachys monieri* 'Hummelo', and *Calamintha nepeta* 'White Cloud', and, at right, massed *Liriope spicata* and *Chamaecyparis pisifera* 'Golden Mop'.

KUN HOUSE 2

RICHARD NEUTRA / LISA GIMMY

LOS ANGELES, CALIFORNIA

The landscape for a famous Neutra House finds new life in a sensitive landscape reimagined by Lisa Gimmy

OPPOSITE Ground cover *Zoysia tenuifolia* acts as a richly textured carpet that also takes care not to obstruct the Neutra house's enviable view; succulents add interest to the rocky foundation below.

Lisa Gimmy saw her first modern landscape when her father took her to see the legendary Sea Ranch on the northern California coast. She was eight years old, but even then the spare, minimalist landscape made an enormous impression. The subliminal lesson: "What you don't do can be as important as what you do."

Decades after this transformative moment (and after considerable education and experience), she is now designing landscapes for some of modern architecture's most significant houses, among them two works by Richard Neutra. In Los Angeles, the architects of the midcentury often built their houses on precipitous sites, which poses plenty of challenges, among them dealing with landslides. It's helpful, then, that the caring new owners of Neutra's Kun House 2, perched on a steep slope near Laurel Canyon, crossed paths with such a studious landscape architect. Gimmy is a devoted student of both the art and history of landscape design as well as a practitioner, so her understanding of Neutra—she calls him "one of the great philosopher-architects of the twentieth century"—is a learned one. She sees this most particularly in terms of his remarkable ability to layer the views through the house and into the landscape, creating a seamless connection between building and nature; she terms it "Neutra's intense engagement with the landscape."

Kun House 2 is so called because it was the second residence Neutra designed for Josef Kun, who was a typesetter at the *Los Angeles Times*; the first, known as Kun House 1, was done in 1936 and is considered to be one of the city's most important prewar modernist landmarks. But fourteen years later, Kun decided to move up the hill a bit and commissioned Neutra to design another house for him. Some six decades later, a new owner hired Gimmy to create a new landscape for

ABOVE A variety of luscious shrubs beautify a practicality: a terraced wall installed to protect against landslides on this steeply sloped site. The shrubs will eventually grow in to conceal the majority of the structure.

RIGHT Boulders and agaves are spaced to allow the sculptural form of each to be appreciated; smaller succulents dot the ground below.

OPPOSITE The boulder wall's craggy rough stones and free-growing succulents are intended as a counterpoint to the pristine rationality of the house's façade.

the second Kun House, which by then was overgrown with vines and had suffered from a landslide that eroded one side of the property.

The Kun House 2 posed a particular challenge because there were no original landscape plans to be found. Thus Gimmy turned to the most appropriate precedent, Neutra's Tremaine House from 1948, which had an original garden from the landscape architect Lockwood de Forest and further work by Ralph Stevens, who took over the job after de Forest's death. Even then, she says, the early plans for the Tremaine House depicted an exciting landscape that ultimately was not executed; instead the plantings pushed too close to the house.

Gimmy opted to "listen to the house and be very quiet," and to maximize and enhance the panoramic view from the house's interior. The first step, however, was to deal with the landslide, with an impact wall and a retaining wall and then build a dry-stack boulder wall of local granite. She planted a variety of gray-green shrubs that will ultimately screen the impact wall and continued the low granite wall around the house, thus creating discrete spaces that, in her words, "juxtapose Neutra's beautiful pristine facade with the rough granite boulders and succulents." Her goal was to use the contrasting textures, colors, and forms to create "a dialectic" while preserving the views.

HARVEY HOUSE

BUFF & HENSMAN, MARMOL RADZINER / MARMOL RADZINER

PALM SPRINGS, CALIFORNIA

A house designed for the actor Laurence Harvey draws drama from a bold new landscape befitting his legacy

OPPOSITE The front of the house is left open to public view, with tufts of *Stipa tenuissima*, sculptural *Fouquieria splendens* behind the low wall and a row of *Parkinsonia* 'Desert Museum' underplanted with red-blooming *Hesperaloe parviflora* along the walk.

"I am fascinated with the total architecture of both house building and movie making," said Laurence Harvey in a 1969 interview shortly after his new house in Palm Springs had been completed. "To make a statement, and make your point, in the simplest possible form is the fine art in both acting and architecture. If there is a simpler way, it is a better way. That's the essence of anything creatively good, really."

In his brief and tumultuous acting career, Harvey was best known for his roles in *The Manchurian Candidate*, *Room at the Top*, *Butterfield 8*, *A Walk on the Wild Side*, and *Summer and Smoke*. The architects Buff & Hensman designed one Hollywood house (in sensibility and site) for Harvey, in Los Angeles, and then this Palm Springs house for him. Decades later, the multitasking Los Angeles design firm of Marmol Radziner undertook a renovation of the gardens there, aiming at both "elevating and refreshing the property" without losing that all-important essence. Marmol Radziner reinforced the hard-edged graphic style in the pool courtyard, used native plants to create a drought-tolerant seasonal garden in the back of the house as an "enhanced desert experience"(removing "thirsty" nonnative palms, rose bushes, and a lawn in the doing), and created a lush oasis in the interior courtyard, a retreat from all that desert dryness. They did retain a small grove of robust citrus trees.

The objective was not so much to mimic the desert-modern style of the midcentury Palm Springs garden, but to update it for a contemporary lifestyle and keep the spirit and attitude of the original period very much alive. In front, the designers chose "beautiful lacy native plants in contrast with the more usual Palm Springs cactus-agave-gravel-rock approach." Walnut doors at the front of the house open directly onto a courtyard that is in turn, transparent. Floor-to-ceiling glass sliders open right back onto the landscape and the pool; the boulders near the pool were in place already. Marmol Radziner kept the existing terrazzo inside and out, and where there was new paving needed, used a concrete aggregate.

Though the 5,500-square-foot house (plus two casitas and a pool cabana) is in very current hands (those of Rea Laccone, cofounder of the fashion brand Vince, and partner Paul Perla) it sits in a neighborhood that comes with well-armed with its own nostalgia, where once Dinah Shore and Kirk Douglas, among others, hid away.

"A house is only four walls," said Harvey in that 1969 interview, which was syndicated to newspapers across the country. "It is the thinking, the planning, the quality put into the design and the materials that make it come alive."

ABOVE A group of Nido chairs by Paola Lenti awaits guests in front of a sinuous Coryphoideae-family palm.

OPPOSITE Boulders that meander along and even into the pool and agaves in various sizes and tones dotted around the perimeter bring the desert landscape into the coutyard. Tall palms are clearly visible above the one-story roofline.

ABOVE A shaded courtyard allows views through floor-to-ceiling glass windows and doors along a bath out to a surprisingly verdant fern grove filled with *Woodwardia fimbriata*.

OPPOSITE A Palm Springs take on a sculpture garden, art courtesy of desert-adapted species each with highly unique forms that play off one another and cause the eye to travel the space by providing interest in varying heights.

WESTOVER HILLS

A. QUINCY JONES, DANIELS AND LOVELADY ARCHITECTURE / HOCKER DESIGN GROUP

DALLAS, TEXAS

In the Westover Hills neighborhood of Fort Worth, a modernist jewel now has a landscape to match its architectural majesty

OPPOSITE Most of the house's windows face the garden, making the dramatic new stair and pool that are accessible from several points in the residence all the more important to adapting the A. Quincy Jones house for contemporary living. Broad risers set into the multipurpose lawn echo the dimensions of the new elements.

In 1966, the Los Angeles architect A. Quincy Jones designed this dramatic house on four acres of terraced hillside in Fort Worth. The original clients were Fran and Eddie Chiles, and it was one of just two houses the famed Southern California modernist designed there. Eddie, an oil baron who owned the Texas Rangers baseball team, died in 1993. The house was eventually left vacant, casting doubts on its future. Fears for the house were abated with a new owner, a meticulous renovation, and a grand new landscape by Hocker Design Group that brings the house back to its modernist roots. It is a complex landscape, a garden of many parts, with still water and moving water, upper terraces and lower terraces, fine materials and some rustic ones. The house, twelve thousand square feet, was carefully renovated by Daniels and Lovelady Architecture, who added a new garage and a pool cabana.

The landscape was reinterpreted, even reinvented, to make house and garden one. Hocker designed a large entry plaza, its proportions based on the grid of the house itself, with the idea that it could accommodate cars and people and be a showcase for art. There is also a reflecting pool, home to koi fish. A walkway of travertine, a beloved midcentury material that can seem fatiguing to today's eye if not used in moderation, crosses the pool. A terrace in back of the house—it is exposed concrete aggregate—also follows the meticulous grid of Jones's architecture and is cooled by prevailing breezes. The grid governs the landscape design in the broad stairway leading to the pool terrace, which Hocker says was a carefully studied "grand architectural gesture."

Within the landscape a private sunken garden leads to a second garden room defined by a granite wall that seems almost carved out of the hillside; a series of water jets spurting through cobblestones creates an interactive fountain here. There is a single continuous path that leads through the property. And despite the apparent "hand of man" here, the plantings are almost entirely created with plants from comparable climates or native species.

LEFT The new, terraced stair includes a water feature and cascading adjacent rill that divides the stairway into two sections—the broader aligns with the edge of the original house's exterior wall.

OPPOSITE An angled granite wall serves as backdrop to waterjets that burble up through cobblestones, one of the house's several water features.

LEFT Mass plantings enhance the house's strong geometry with their clean lines and sharp divisions between ground cover, eye-height palms, and tree canopy overhead. A hydrangea injects a blousy moment to catch the eye.

OPPOSITE A new circular drive and travertine entry plaza functions practically as a drop-off area and aesthetically as a showcase for art.

PRESENT PERFECT

NEW LANDSCAPES THAT EXPOUND AND EXPAND THE IDEAS OF MIDCENTURY ARCHITECTURE

When a house is imagined as an object in the landscape, it is often just that. Philip Johnson's Glass House in New Canaan acquired its landscape, mostly in the form of eccentric modernist follies, over the years. Mies van der Rohe's Farnsworth House was basically set in nature, as was often the case with modernist houses, especially those built where there was once forest—or farmland or craggy rocks. Though built for a life in which land and building were one, that was not always, not even often, the case. The pace of building was fast, demand high, and more often than not, even important modernist houses by important modernist architects were turned over to their first owners without much more than a few trees, or in the desert, a few cacti.

This can mean a blank slate, an opportunity to envision what could have been there instead of recapturing the past. In areas where there are climate and environmental considerations, it is also an opportunity to build for the future using drought-tolerant plants in water-parched California, for example, or eliminating exotics in favor of far less greedy natives. It is also an opportunity to envision what could have been and to let the landscape make the architecture soar, and vice versa.

HILLSIDE MODERN WITH A VIEW

HOWARD B. ZOOK, EMILY FARNHAM / TERREMOTO

PASADENA, CALIFORNIA

A vibrant new landscape by Terremoto brings out the best in a carefully restored ranch house

OPPOSITE Expansive floor-to-ceiling windows open wide at several points to allow access to the yard even while plants do the work of screening all those windows from outside eyes.

This 1950s ranch house designed by the fine but little-known midcentury architect Harold B. Zook in Pasadena had been altered (the kind word for it is "insensitively"), but its new owners—the singer and actress Mandy Moore and her then-fiancé, musician Taylor Goldsmith—saw its potential. They hired the Los Angeles architect Emily Farnham, who in turn hired the landscape architecture firm Terremoto, which is led by David Godshall.

Farnham took on the task of returning the house to its original architectural intent, working with Zook's original plans and restoring elements that had been lost along the way to create an elegant, low-lying jewel of a house. Terremoto also confronted a dated, decrepit hardscape that had evolved over the decades and was neither original nor true to the architecture, introducing a new landscape that turned out surprisingly to be close to the original, unrealized design intent. Says Godshall, "it was essentially an infrastructural tabula rasa." It was in the course of research that the designers stumbled upon an original landscape plan that had never been executed; it was basically the same plan as Terremoto's, proving any number of clichés to be correct (great minds, stars aligned).

At the beginning of the project, the landscape was what Godshall called a "nonlinear mashup" of oak trees, a madrone tree, a mature sycamore, and an array of Australian plants. Terremoto saved the trees and added in what he calls a "native-ish" garden with banks of flowering plants including bougainvillea and salvia along with cactus and agave. "It was clear that someone (or multiple people) who had occupied the house at some point in time cared about plants," Godshall says. "Landscape projects on existing homes are often editorial in nature and this was no exception. We identify what works, what doesn't, and we react and adjust accordingly."

The house wasn't perfectly orthogonal, and Godshall found that "it reacted to the site in a thoughtful, pleasant way. We like to ground our projects with a conceptual basis, so Diego Lopez (of Terremoto) and I spent some time with tracing

paper, dreaming and riffing and chatting. Feeling the plan out." They chose a grid, in part because it is an "eternal unit" but also because it is "entirely appropriate and comfortable with midcentury modern architecture," he says. Terremoto overlaid grids of various scale to reflect the weight of the garden's purpose. Thus the driveway grid is large, the pool grid medium sized, and the more intimate areas small—though there is a moment where all three grids "collide" in a visual focal point. The pool was also rebuilt. A long, low, custom-designed bench now lines one side; a pergola shades an outdoor dining area opposite. There's also a firepit for cooler evenings.

LEFT An existing sycamore receives an underplanting of *Verbena bonariensis*, a cardoon, and low grasses, all set in warm decomposed gravel that echoes the tone of the mountains beyond.

OPPOSITE A low brick planter filled with a row of grasses keeps views out and open while allowing the seed heads to wave gently just above the sill.

ABOVE A minimalist bench unobtrusively lines one side of the pool, coordinating with the gravel, while opuntia dotted throughout pick up on the darker tones of the sycamore's peeling bark.

OPPOSITE A mature madrone in a fresh bed planted with grasses and agaves anchors the pool patio; lounge chairs upholstered in wear-resistant black sit at the ready for days of splashing and admiring the view.

NEW CANAAN MIDCENTURY MODERN

JOHN BLACK LEE, JOEL SANDERS / WAGNER HODGSON

NEW CANAAN, CONNECTICUT

Important modernist precedents help create a new setting for a renovated and enlarged jewel

OPPOSITE Broad stripes of *Sedum spurium* 'Dragon's Blood' border an even wider planting of *Carex morrowii* 'Ice Dance' that faces the center of the house, bringing geometry to the garden that's a match for the classic midcentury architecture.

The architect John Black Lee, who died in 2016 at the age of 91, was sometimes called the "sixth member" of New Canaan's famous group of architects known as the Harvard Five, who filled the rolling wooded hills there with important works of modernist architecture. Lee was slightly younger than the others, had gone to Brown University rather than Harvard, and didn't establish his practice in New Canaan until 1954—though the town was still in its architectural heyday then.

Like so many of his New Canaan counterparts, starting with Philip Johnson and his Glass House, Lee often saw his houses as objects floating in the landscape rather than being rooted in—and part of—the land. This was indeed the case with this 1957 house, which was renovated and added to by Joel Sanders and then given a powerful and poetic landscape by Dale Schafer of Wagner Hodgson Landscape Architects.

"This was a hidden gem," he says, "surrounded by traditional houses and not in the woods, just kind of sitting there." The stylistic (and philosophical) disconnect with the rest of its neighborhood called for screening the nearly three-acre site, in this case with evergreens.

Schafer began working without precedents but felt compelled to work in the idiom of the era, intimately connecting the house and the landscape. "I tried to keep the planting within the genre of the time," he says. He turned to Dan Kiley's Miller Garden for inspiration. "I wanted there to be a tapestry to look out on without a lot of fussiness."

He added a teardrop-shaped driveway and created a parking area that interspersed planting and paving to add visual interest. The parking area is separated from the rest of the grounds by a Cor-Ten steel blade fence that allows you to emerge from your car and glimpse the garden on the other side. That wall and a second one, made of bluestone, help define the landscape into four distinct quadrants.

The plantings themselves were done with an eye to color and contrast, in swaths of saturated hues that are separate one from one another. The design forms a kind of living

carpet—taking its cues from the Miller House in imparting the sense of an outdoor room—that from a greater distance seems as if it could be a color field painting. Schafer did not shy away from flowering shrubs and trees; there are dogwoods, rhododendron, hydrangeas, and magnolias, among many other others, letting the garden glow in a range of reds, oranges, purples, and lavenders, among other hues.

The house's new "great room," added by Sanders, has walls of glass that open directly out onto the "carpeted outdoor room." It's definitely an East Coast garden, Schafer says—more formalized, but one that has deep philosophical roots in the precepts of midcentury landscape design.

ABOVE The drive patterned with turf joints between precast pavers is lined with a trim hedge of *Taxus baccata* 'Repandens'. Vertical posts create an ornamental screen fence that successfully indicates a border at the top while allowing views through to the garden beyond; it's underplanted with *Euonymus fortunei* 'Colorata'. All emphasize and accentuate the horizontal and vertical lines and proportions of the original house.

OPPOSITE The view to the garden from the interior shows how carefully the proportions of the block planting are keyed to the proportions of the house's frame; the tree is also low enough to be framed entirely by the floor-to-ceiling windows, without breaking the plane of the roofline.

CONANT HOUSE

RICHARD BARANCIK, MARGARET McCURRY / MARIA SMITHBURG

GLENVIEW, ILLINOIS

Near Chicago, a sensitive update gives this house even deeper connections to its garden

OPPOSITE The house's owners tell people it's designed with such a good flow they often have to explain to guests where one area stops and another begins; were it not for the glass, the same could be said of the transparency from inside to out. Planting beds wrap the full exterior, integrating the open structure directly into the landscape.

"I always like to unfold the garden inside the house," says the landscape architect Maria Smithburg of her design for the Conant House in Glenview, just north of Chicago. The house itself was a jewel, designed in 1953 by Richard Barancik and attentively renovated and expanded by the architect Margaret McCurry. After the death of the original owners, Howard and Doris Conant, the house remained in the family, passing on to the next generation.

McCurry's mandates were severalfold: to update the house for future generations (in part, as a safeguard against demolition), bring the wood and stone back to their original luster, brighten the interiors, and connect it more closely with nature.

The house was designed for that intimate link to nature, with stone floors and even walls, wood ceilings, and panoramic windows, but there were more opportunities to amplify the connection. By the time the renovation was complete, the lines between inside and out had become blurred enough that the journalist Joseph Giovannini suggested that the house encouraged the Conant children to be kids "because it fooled them into thinking they were outside when they were inside."

In her renovation, McCurry was able to match the wood and the Tennessee limestone, which was still being quarried. She opened up the kitchen, replaced outdated lighting, and added more glass, including skylights ("all of a sudden, it glowed," she says. In general, she was able to open the house to the views that include not just the immediate landscape but also the Cook County Forest Preserve beyond. "The landscape evolves," says McCurry. "It is more formal close to the house and becomes more naturalistic as you get closer to the woods."

Smithburg, who is also an architect by training and whose firm is called Artemisia, sought to tie the landscape to the architecture by bringing "shapes, form, and texture" to it, selecting shrubs that had architectural properties and trees, such as sumac and yucca, that are more sculptural. She used a "reddish-brownish" gravel to pair with the stone floors and walls. She included river birch in the mix because, she says, "the bark looks like stone." A key goal was to make it a garden for four seasons, no small feat in the often-harsh Chicago climate. "It is very green in summer," she says, "then reddish-gold in the fall. In the spring there are fields of bluebells, like a sea of water."

LEFT, ABOVE Views and warm stone run through the house, inside and out; a low exterior planter holds specimen plants that can peek in on diners.

LEFT, BELOW A green curtain for bath privacy is an enviable kind.

OPPOSITE Even at night, subtle lighting outside and light permeating out from inside sources throw the sculptural forms of the varied plantings into sharp relief.

PASADENA MODERN

NORD ERIKSSON

PASADENA, CALIFORNIA

A garden for a midcentury ranch house embraces the region's Mediterranean climate and pays homage to the designer's modernist father

OPPOSITE Simple terracing and hardscape in lines that parallel the house's orientation create a sense of harmony; contemporary elements were added while protecting a mature cork oak (*Quercus suber*) on site.

Nord Eriksson's South Pasadena home is a 1949 ranch house, modest and low-lying, but true to form it opens onto the landscape—in this case a sequence of garden rooms that embrace the long views of Pasadena's high perch over the city of Los Angeles. "The back story to the house," he says, "is that I know almost nothing about it. There's a beautiful set of drawings, but they aren't signed." The landscape architect Edward Huntsman-Trout left original drawings that Eriksson says were "very sparse."

Eriksson is a second-generation landscape architect. He quite literally learned at his father's feet, tagging along to job sites with his father, who gave him "a love of using our local materials—concrete, indigenous stone." His decades as a practitioner have helped him to see that timelessness, rather than chasing trends, is the smart way to design. His philosophy developed along the way—ideas that include letting the garden unfold slowly so that there's a sense of mystery to it. "I'm a huge believer in creating mystery . . . whenever possible gardens should unfold. I've observed that with what you can't see, say a part of a garden behind a hedge, your mind assumes what it wants to, and this often makes the garden feel larger," he says.

Now a principal in EPT Design, the firm his father founded early in the 1960s, Eriksson has, in his own home, a perfect laboratory to explore ideas about gardens and landscape. While his father looked at design through a lens of modernism, he says he has found looking back "to be deeply relevant and the best work I do has its feet in history, the present, and the future."

When Eriksson and his family moved into the house in 2000, the back garden was basically bare—a big stone patio with a high rock wall, a rose garden, brick paths, and a lawn that sloped down to the edge. Eriksson changed that to keep the patio but without the high view-obscuring wall and broad steps of concrete, with troughs of river rock leading to a set of terraced rooms. There are surfaces of gravel, cobble, and flagstone, and a raised "conversation pad" made of salvaged pieces of concrete. The greatest expanse of the garden includes a swimming pool that is bordered with stone from the lowered wall. Off to one side is a smaller garden room.

If site and geography inform the landscape, it is also informed in equal, likely greater, measure by a trip to Spain that Eriksson and his family took as a part of a monthlong sabbatical (each of the partners of EPK Design takes one), where he observed—and was wowed by—the drought-tolerant

gardens he saw in a country where the climate is much like that of Southern California, with short and rainy winters and long, hot, dry summers. He took copious notes while he was there and then back home, translated those thoughts onto a letter-size piece of paper that he still refers to today, his planting bible. "Everything I saw holds together, still today," he says. "I didn't premeditate to take a deep look at the Spanish gardens relative to the work I do in a similar climate but fell into a deep observation of the parallels almost instantly upon arrival in Madrid. Over the month, which included time in Madrid, Seville, Granada, Malaga, and the island of Mallorca, I became convinced that certain plants were thriving in extreme conditions. I spent much of the month taking stock. Water is scarce in Spain, as it is in California. I was really amazed at the use of cisterns to capture and hold water and then release it into gardens via gravity-fed channels."

The palette of the garden thus reflects that Mediterranean sensibility (which is also a Southern California sensibility) with blue-greens, gray-greens, and pops of color from mallow and Nepeta. Pots assembled over the years hold a variety of cacti, as well as other succulents and aloes, and more, the collecting a habit he acquired as his father's sidekick when he was young. "I tend to like things that I've found a piece at a time . . . and find the ways that they are harmonious and then group accordingly," he says. "I love the sense of time and history that this represents. Most of what I have has a story. That early instinct to pick up pieces at my dad's job sites seems to translate into finding little gems at garage sales and flea markets, deals from retailers, or castoffs from clients. All of that said, I'm also careful to avoid clutter. Every once in a while I edit and purge just to keep things from getting too busy."

RIGHT A large and prominently placed *Agave americana* acts as garden art.

OPPOSITE The purple blooms of *Lavatera maritima* and creeping thyme accent the blue-gray tones of the garden's retaining wall while adding delicate blossoms and foliage.

FAR LEFT A simple metal ring leans intriguingly against a tree trunk while *Pelargonium tomentosum* busies itself with growing through its base.

LEFT The dancing flames in a fire pit emulate the whimsical reaches of a *Cereus jamacaru* cactus just behind.

OPPOSITE The branches of the front yard's mature tree hover just above the roofline, allowing the house to greet the street while the plantings at ground level, including a range of textures from the broad, variegated leaves of a giant agave to the small, waving seedheads of grasses and the craggy outlines of boulders, draw the eye.

MIDCENTURY MAKEOVER

EUGENE KINN CHOY / LISA GIMMY

LOS ANGELES, CALIFORNIA

A landscape in Los Feliz honors its architectural pedigree while fulfilling the outdoor-living dreams of a young family

OPPOSITE A white retaining wall throws the subtle variations of the blue-green agaves and shrubs above into relief; *Rosmarinus officinalis* 'Huntington Carpet' trails over the top. Newly installed broad stairs are set in gravel that can, when necessary, create a pervious surface to absorb rainwater.

Eugene Kinn Choy was among the first Chinese-American architects to practice in Los Angeles, and he left behind a celebrated body of work, including the landmark Cathay Bank Building. His houses were then and are now sought-after gems of early modernism. With its sandstone cladding and strong proportions, this particular house in Los Feliz, dating to 1952, is a noteworthy addition to his archive.

For landscape architect Lisa Gimmy, there were a lot of "facts on the ground," including the house, the pool house, and the pool. There were also the realities of the steep slope of the backyard, a retaining wall that was crumbling, drainage issues, and what Gimmy termed "a monoculture" of Algerian ivy.

The new owners wanted to expand outdoors to gain additional living and dining space. A key intervention was to grade the sloping lot to create two levels, thus two discrete spaces, separating them with broad, "generous" stairs. Gimmy also replaced the retaining wall to bring it up to code, planting the top of the slope with drought-tolerant agaves, succulents, and shrubs, and softening it with fragrant trailing rosemary and pots full of colorful succulents. The stairs and new terraces were designed to seem to float within bands of gravel, thus giving them an aesthetic subtlety and solving drainage problems by providing water catchment and infiltration.

The house opens wide onto its new landscape, and in good weather, its owners, Catherine Dupree and M-K O'Connell, often keep it wide open, fulfilling their ambition of a house that flows from inside to out.

RIGHT Rounded agaves reflect the curved shape of the entry stairs; the gravel chosen as mulch pairs with the tones of the original stonework. Plantings in front are kept deliberately simple so as not to compete with Neutra's architecture.

OPPOSITE, ABOVE The decking and furniture around the pool is minimal, in keeping with the lines of the house. Containers holding a variety of succulents add dimension at patio level.

OPPOSITE, BELOW Neutra designed sliding doors that open almost the full width of the living room to allow indoor/outdoor flow; the garden beyond is designed to provide visual interest when seen from the interior by providing plantings at ground level, eye height, and a tree canopy to lead the eye to the hillside beyond.

BALCONES HOUSE

R. GOMMEL ROESSNER, CLAYTON & LITTLE / WORD AND CARR DESIGN GROUP

AUSTIN, TEXAS

A house and garden by a Texas visionary is renovated to honor the past and live in the present

OPPOSITE Massive Texas live oaks are allowed pride of place and maintained so as not to collide with the roofline. Simple grasses and a few patio pots are all else that's needed to embellish the main entry.

Today little known outside Texas, even outside of Austin, R. Gommel Roessner was a daring and visionary modernist who taught at the University of Texas School of Architecture from 1948 to 1982, and in his day, his work attracted national and international notice. This house, completed in 1964, was among his notable achievements, particularly for its rich use of copper, glass, handmade brick, and redwood. Roessner was known for his ability to reflect a Southwestern aesthetic in his nonetheless fully modernist houses.

This house, on a hilly site in Austin's Balcones neighborhood, was renovated by the architectural firm of Clayton & Little, led in this case by Emily Little. For the landscape, the Austin-based Word and Carr began by editing out the brushy overgrowth that had built up around the mature oaks over the years. "There is a stacked limestone retaining wall at the foot of the house, running under the balcony, that the design team felt contributed strongly to the identity of the house," says Sarah Carr. "It was a struggle to keep but well worth the effort in the end." A "challenger" oak tree whose life was threatened by the wall—it was girdling the tree's roots—was saved by the selective demolition of a piece of the wall, but the rest was saved and restored. "The loveliest element of the property is without a doubt the live oak canopy we inherited. We made an effort to keep the number of the species low in each given space to preserve the quiet focus on these trees," says Carr.

Added to that are oak leaf hydrangea, dwarf yaupon, and sandy leaf fig that buffer the lawn from the street and a pea gravel parking area. The garden edge of the walk is planted with three species of drought-tolerant fern, crinum lilies, Japanese maple, and, says Carr, "a very interesting tiny-leafed ligustrum shrub."

Word and Carr built a new stone-and-concrete stairway that leads from the street to the front door, and a new swimming pool. The driveway was raised to accommodate the decades of growth of tree roots. An entry courtyard with concrete pavers in a square grid with redwood dividers was not in good shape; this was replaced by poured concrete that was, Carr says, "etched and saw-cut into a grid pattern to honor the initial intent." A new walkway from the street to the house reiterates the tapered profile of the house's cantilevered balcony.

Rather than a strict restoration, the owners of this important house wanted to honor the past in a house that met present-day needs. "Preserving the feel of the house, the trees, and the neighborhood character were our main goals," says Carr. "We owe much to the house itself, which is a wonder.

The scale and siting of it are just perfection. It manages to be modest, efficient, and gracious while also expansive in its outlook and absolutely luxurious.

"There's something almost shy about the way it reveals itself by degrees. It was important to us that the garden spaces be imbued with the same qualities. To that end we resolved not to introduce new materials, showy colors, or anything that couldn't have plausibly been part of the property when the house when new.

"The magic of this project, to me, is that it's such an example of what is possible. Preserving a house of this scale so beautifully is the ultimate reproach to all the bloated McMansions out there. I imagine what the street must have felt like fifty and sixty years ago with these thoughtful houses, set back far from the street, tucked into the trees. Not one thing screaming for attention."

RIGHT A stacked limestone retaining wall original to the house needed to be restored and resized to stop hindering the growth of nearby tree roots.

OPPOSITE As part of the emphasis on revealing the house by degrees, a simple courtyard adorned with an intricate rock provides a moment of pause; live oaks amply fill in the sky overhead.

RIGHT The front walk climbs the hill with a unique combination of rough-hewn stone and smooth concrete. The materials match the Southwestern warmth of the original building while the whole remains very recognizably modernist.

OPPOSITE A new plunge pool and simple Acapulco chairs provide the opportunity for a private dip, secreted as it is in a courtyard.

BRILLHART MIAMI MODERN

JAKE AND MELISSA BRILLHART

MIAMI, FLORIDA

In a tucked-away urban neighborhood near the Miami River, a new house explores decades-old ideas about connecting architecture and nature

OPPOSITE The house features fifty feet of uninterrupted glass on each side, and four sets of sliding glass doors to open the interiors to the elements completely while shutters along both façades offer privacy and protection from the elements while allowing breezes. Ferns, bromeliads, and subtropical ground covers fill in the gap between the ground and the house's base, elevated five feet.

Architects Jacob and Melissa Brillhart took what they call a "back-to-basics" approach to the making of this airy, open new house. As a young married couple, they knew that their own house would be a hands-on project. They had also studied older architectural models searching for precedent. Says Melissa, "We asked ourselves what was necessary; how could we minimize our impact on the earth; how do we respect the context of the neighborhood; and what can we really build?"

Some of the answers came from familiar sources, says Jacob, "the seemingly forgotten American vernacular, and more specifically, the 'dog trot,' which for well over a century, has been a dominant image representing Florida 'cracker' architecture." Historically speaking, the "dog trot" house was two small (almost always wood) buildings connected to one another by a central breezeway—all of it under a single roof. "This simple, practical building is both modest and rich in cultural meaning; maximizes efficiency, space, and energy; relies on vernacular building materials; and celebrates the breezes."

The Brillharts capitalized on this time-tested form, creating a house with a floor plan that is a modern interpretation of the dog trot house, with sleeping quarters one side, a central corridor (with kitchen), and then living space on the other side. A second model for the house (though it too draws on American vernacular) is the modernist Florida house. The Brillharts looked at the work of such postwar modernists in Florida as Paul Rudolph, Alfred Browning Parker, and Mark Hampton, architects who, in their eyes, "gave birth to a tropical modern school of thought and developed their own regional interpretations of the International Style by turning to local landscape, climate and materials to inform their designs." They employed technology and creative construction techniques, among other innovations. Using precedents as inspiration, they sought to go forward by looking back, and further to seek an alternative to the concrete house ubiquitous in Florida today.

The Brillhart house is made of glass, steel, and shiplapped wood (on the exterior sustainable ipe wood, which is highly suited for tropical climates) along with western red cedar used in the sixteen shuttered doors. (Interior woods are white oak and cypress on the floor and American cherry for the cabinetry.) It sits in the Spring Garden Historic District, one of Miami's oldest neighborhoods, which means that unlike much of South Florida, wood is a prevalent building material and homes there take cues from both location and landscape. The house is raised five feet about the ground, not just to

meet the dictates of contemporary building codes but also to anticipate Florida's inevitable rising waters. An additional (and not secondary) motive was the desire to sit lightly on the land. The house is designed to be part of the tropics, with what Jacob terms "varying levels of transparency." The entrance is jungle-like and opaque and then opens up. The house is designed with wooden shutters, louvers, sliding glass doors, and open-air porches to make it part of, not separate from, the landscape.

This last was a dominant goal of the design, to create a house that had an immediate relationship with the surrounding landscape. "Because of that, the selection of flora became as important to the architectural experience as the structure itself," says Melissa. The couple selected ten different palms and an array of trees, many of them natives, along with shrubs, low plants, and ground cover.

"The integration of low-tech sustainability measures that were reliant on natural systems received great attention as well," she says. "Working with a limited budget, we did most of the landscaping ourselves! We were also interested in developing a sequence of experiences, beginning with the entry. The idea was to enter through a small wooden gate at the street, and then walk through a dense forest before coming on axis to the house."

LEFT Local stone and wood continue the theme of celebrating Florida's regional and vernacular for this entry gate, whose design previews the house's slatted shutters.

OPPOSITE The narrow dog trot–style house still features eight hundred square feet of patio space, along with floor-to-ceiling glass walls. The importance of the dense native plantings outside as both wallpaper to the interiors and as a critical element for privacy is clear.

MIRAMAR RESIDENCE

OGLESBY GREEN / HOCKER DESIGN GROUP

HIGHLAND PARK, TEXAS

A new build that sits thoughtfully and well in its historic neighborhood

OPPOSITE This new-construction house sits on a corner lot at an intersection; the first order of business for the planting is to shield it from passersby.

Corner houses are, in general, desirable real estate, but from the point of view of the landscape designer, they can pose their own issues. This particular house in the Dallas suburb of Highland Park sits at an intersection where one street is busy with cars and another that is pedestrian-friendly—thus the challenge. Highland Park is also a close-in suburban neighborhood known for its hedge-lined streets and gracious homes, so the intervention needed to fit the context.

Hocker's solution was to create a foreground defined by dense planting along ivy-twined courtyard walls which—though the house is thoroughly modern, invoking the best tenets of mid-twentieth-century architecture, makes it seem as if it had been there for decades. The idea was to conceal the house from the traffic and at the same time seem inviting to pedestrians by reinterpreting the age-old Hispano-Moresque courtyard, which anchors it to its leafy surroundings.

The landcape architects' goal was to make the house seem not brand new, but more, an integral part of the neighbhood—a goal achieved by enshrouding the exterior courtyard walls in greenery and creating a fully permeable cobbled drive seeded with dichondra so that it not only has a patina of time but also seems part of the garden. The landscape, too, imparts the idea of permanence with mature trees and a first floor that is intimately connected to the garden.

Inside those walls are a pool and spa, along with a guest house connected to the main house via a series of outdoor rooms. Key elements are Pennsylvania bluestone along with a series of reflective pools. Woodland plants, boulders, and birch take the site from hardscape to a more bucolic landscape, an escape from the bustle outside the courtyard walls. Inside those walls, the Hocker group sought to maintain the neighborhood ethos of sustainability by regarding the yard as an urban woodland and filling it with live oak, cedar elm, ginkgo, Japanese maple, and saucer magnolia—all presiding over an undergrowth that includes purple wintercreeper accented with ferns.

The goals here were noble ones: to make the property an integral part of the neighborhood while ensuring the privacy of interior spaces, including the pool and the guest house. A second and more private woodland with benches and a fire pit all made from local stone allows the homeowners and their guests to gaze out the manmade wild of wood fern, southern river fern, Chinese indigo, limelight hydrangea, cast iron plant and dichondra. Throughout, Hocker relied on both native and adapted plants, but the ultimate goal was to create a showcase for resilient design

ABOVE The peeling, red-toned bark of river birches adds texture at eye level in this side yard; the tone is picked up as well by a rustic firepit and nearby bench. Asymmetric pavers interplanted with low-growing ground cover also indicate that this is an informal part of the garden.

RIGHT Walls covered in vertical verdure do an excellent job of screening the house behind from the street as well as helping it to feel immediately established in the neighborhood.

LEFT Efforts made to interlace pavers with low ground cover and to allow plants to cascade blousily over the edges of paths are meant to signal that the house has been a part of the neighborhood for decades, effectively concealing its recent vintage.

OPPOSITE A spa tucked between the contemplative side courtyard and the main pool deck is placed as deeply as possible into the site for privacy.

3801

RIGHT Low shrubs and smooth stairs lead to the main pool deck; the retaining wall's "windows" help the two spaces to stay connected, visually, while still indicating a transition in programmatic uses.

OPPOSITE Allées of trees and plentiful ground covers create a pleasant welcome to the house's main entrance, necessarily screened off from the bustling street adjacent.

FOUND OBJECTS

LANDSCAPES THAT TRANSFORM MIDCENTURY HOUSES FROM ORDINARY TO EXTRAORDINARY

In 1951, Olan G. and Aida T. Hafley commissioned Richard Neutra to design a modest house in Long Beach, California. Aida Hafley had read an article about Neutra in *Time* magazine, and Olan recalled learning about the then-young architect in a civics class in high school in Illinois. The couple had planned on interviewing several architects, but they saw Neutra first, and "his personality was so dynamic and his interest in our needs and wants so intense that thoughts of anyone else faded and we commissioned him on the spot," she later said. It was a small two-story house, built side by side with a second, even more unassuming Neutra house. Both were built with the humblest of materials—plywood, Masonite, Formica, wood veneer, plastic laminate, aluminum.

Fast-forward six decades, plus. By then, the two Neutra houses (the second one had been designed for the portrait painter Bethuel C. Moore) sat almost unnoticed in a neighborhood filled with custom-designed houses, largely from later in the twentieth century and mostly one-story with broad, overhanging rooflines. The Hafleys continued to live there until 2010, when Aida died. Then new owners came in, committed to preservation—and did it right, top to bottom.

It might be an exaggeration, but chances are there's at least one such hidden jewel in almost every neighborhood of any even slightly mature age—the stray modern house that has been ignored for decades. Usually it has good bones, maybe even an architectural pedigree. Often it's been loved, just allowed to languish. Sometimes they've been altered or expanded beyond recognition. But these are the houses that midcentury dreams are made of—and great gardens. In the hands of a good designers, these diamonds in the rough can become polished (and valued, and valuable) jewels.

HAFLEY HOUSE

RICHARD NEUTRA / LISA GIMMY

LONG BEACH, CALIFORNIA

As part of an award-winning restoration team, Lisa Gimmy creates a garden worthy of a small house by Richard Neutra

OPPOSITE The square pavers set into gravel are a feature original to the garden, and have been retained; *Agave attenuata* and *Yucca rostrata* are new additions. A *Callistemon viminalis* adds height.

The Hafley House was built in 1953, one of two side-by-side homes Richard Neutra designed in the comparatively modest Long Beach midcentury neighborhood of Park Estates. The Hafley and Moore houses show a similar aesthetic in terms of massing and materials, as well as in their connection to nature, though the former is two stories and the latter just one. This 2,081-square-foot structure remained in a single ownership, that of Olan and Aida Hafley, from 1953 through 2010. The new owners decided to restore it, and did so in award-winning fashion, assembling a "dream team" that included the preservation architect Kelly Sutherlin McLeod as well as conservator John Griswold, and Neutra scholar Barbara Lambrecht—and for the landscape, Lisa Gimmy. The work has garnered awards from the international modernist preservation advocacy organization Docomomo as well as from the Los Angeles Conservancy.

The existing trees and shrubs were in bad shape and could not be saved, so among Gimmy's goals was to create a drought-tolerant landscape that required minimal maintenance and respected the Morse House next door. Though she had only a rough site plan that showed an unbuilt swimming pool to work from, they did have correspondence that included Neutra, the contractor, and the Hafleys. She was also able to look at the array of Julius Shulman photos available in the Getty and Shulman family archives, as well as the Hafleys' own family album, which contained color photos of the site.

Some of the existing hardscape elements could be preserved, she found, including the concrete paving that led from the living room out to the garden. Correspondence showed that the Hafleys ran low on funds and finished the job themselves, relying on Neutra's written instructions. In Gimmy's hands, the garden seems equally rooted in Neutra's philosophy and aesthetic and contemporary needs.

Sliding doors open seamlessly onto a patio. The original hardscape was expanded to provide, as Gimmy says, "a new paradigm for a neighborhood dominated by large areas of turf." The original concrete walkway to the front door was preserved as was the living room terrace, which was further defined by the addition of *Dracaena marginata*. The trees in decline were replaced by drought-tolerant alternatives. There is a flowering trumpet vine tree, *Tecoma stans*, in the courtyard. A gravel area framed by boulders is not intended, as some might conclude "to create a naturalistic effect of a river bed or stream, rather, to act as a graphic foreground to the architecture," she says. Where there is lawn, it is "low mow," drought-tolerant grass—part of the wider effort to celebrate Neutra's before-its-time ecological architecture.

RIGHT A waterwise garden that provides abundant verdure for Long Beach includes *Yucca rostrata*, *Agave attenuata*, and *Euphorbia rigida*.

OPPOSITE Tufts of grass *Juncus effusus* 'Elk Blue' outline the path, leading the way into the house, while an *Agonis flexuosa* reaches to the second-story windows, providing visible green to the upper level's interior spaces.

LEFT Neutra's focus on indoor/outdoor living is apparent, as main living spaces are designed to flow directly and easily into the garden.

OPPOSITE A sunny patio with simple butterfly chairs, agaves and *Pedilanthus bracteatus* dotted around, and sculptural rocks are a recipe for relaxation.

1501

KEY WEST TRANSFORMATION

ROB DELAUNE / RAYMOND JUNGLES

KEY WEST, FLORIDA

In Key West, the boundaries of a 1940 ranch-style house go from inside to out, fulfilling the dream of life in the subtropics

OPPOSITE The entry sequence includes a carport, trellis, and gate. The travertine pavers lead directly back to the water garden.

The southernmost city in the United States, Key West is known for its array of century-old Queen Anne style architecture, houses with cupolas and bay windows and lots of filigree trim. But the house that Susan Henshaw Jones and her husband, Richard Eaton, bought there as a winter getaway was nondescript at best—a plain, one-story 1940s structure. In the hands of landscape architect Raymond Jungles, this straightforward suburban-like house was transformed into tropical paradise where the boundaries between architecture and nature dissolved.

Jungles worked with Key West architect Rob Delaune to design interior spaces that span the lot from property line to property line with pocket doors that disappear into the walls and open onto the gardens, transforming house and garden into a single space. An atrium brings sunlight to the house's inner reaches. The landscape includes a walkway that seems to float above a water garden and a fountain that is fed by a small pump, as well as a new swimming pool.

The master bedroom opens onto the garden. There's a perforated garden wall that offers glimpses of the garden that gives privacy to the spare bedroom wing. The landscape uses the entire site to the utmost.

Jungles chose plants that were appropriate for the subtropical site, emphasizing both for their beauty and their lack of thirst; the plantings, primarily native, include a layer of trees that screen the house from its neighbors and provide a habitat for local birds.

For Jungles it was a chance to express ideas about the connections between architecture and nature that he had long been exploring. It was also an opportunity, he says, to enhance the family's lifestyle and create a space that elevates the role of both art and nature.

RIGHT Garden architecture as well as furnishings endow this 1940s house with a decidedly midcentury mood. The dense subtropical plantings screen the yard effectively from neighbors; a casual observer would never realize that the water wall and water garden are only ten feet from the property line.

OPPOSITE The trellis supports herald's trumpet and jacquemontia vines.

LEFT Water trickles down a sloped concrete chute and into the fifty-foot lap pool; the planters above are punctuated by the orange leaves of an aechmea.

ABOVE The water garden, on the opposite side of the house from the pool, shares travertine pavers as a consistent element that ties various programmatic areas together.

OPPOSITE Travertine panels floating in the water garden are designed to provide refuge for fish swimming below; the hue of the sculptural fountain provides depth of color beyond what even the lush subtropical plantings that surround it can provide.

KANSAS CITY "IDEA HOUSE"

WILLIAM WURSTER, FORWARD DESIGN | ARCHITECTURE / PLAID COLLABORATIVE

MISSION HILLS, KANSAS

A 1957 "model" house—the product of a California case study architect—gains new life and new utility in a renovation that offers strong connections inside and out.

OPPOSITE Neat rows of shrubs lined with *Hakonechloa macra* 'Aureola' along the entry walkway underscore the quintessential midcentury lines of the house. Two *Cercis canadensis* 'Alba' provide white blooms in spring and red foliage in fall.

Chris Fein was asked by his clients, who were downsizing, to restore, renovate, and adapt a modest house in the Kansas City suburb of Mission Hills. It was a house with a lively story behind it. Designed by the renowned San Francisco modern architect William Wurster (1895–1973), it had been a 1957 *Better Homes and Gardens* Idea Home of the Year, which meant that not only did it embrace ideas that were ahead of their time, but also it was a spec house. The house was "relatively bare bones," says Fein, but the magazine article gave him a springboard for the update.

It had a single owner for almost sixty years. "At the point we started it was a great house with great bones but it showed its age both on the exterior and interior," says Fein, whose firm is the Kansas City–based Forward Design | Architecture. "Our approach overall was to extend the house in a way that would, for lack of a better term, be an 'invisible hand.' That is to say we wanted the exterior work to look as though nothing had ever been done."

One key—true to the ethos of postwar modernism—was to enhance the interior view in each direction through the house into the landscape of the side yard. This was done by changing the axis of the master bedroom and adding courtyards.

To create the landscape design, Forward worked with Plaid Collaborative, also based in Kansas City. The objective was to keep the landscape strong and simple, with controlled views and a refined plant palette that works to both define spaces and soften the edges.

"The overall goal was to find a landscape design that was sympathetic to the house and climate," says Fein. The solution was to create some outdoor spaces that were secluded for privacy and others that were open and public where warranted. Using bluestone and ipe, Wurster's original entry court was extended with the addition of a space that functions and a raised portion that could be used as a traditional front porch is, for sitting and talking.

On the rear of the house the designers enlarged a back terrace. An extended ipe-wood deck and lower bluestone fire pit patio reach from both the kitchen and living room, offering outdoor living space for the family; in turn, the deck opens up onto a raised, but flattened, "lawn terrace."

Fein created a courtyard between the master bedroom and the garage to allow for "a view to nature that is still private in a typical mid century suburban context." A second courtyard, long and skinny, is reached through a reorganized guest room.

The garden includes a bosque of Japanese maple trees, as well as several yew, holly, cedar, various grasses, and the dwarf variegated boxwood that border the front of the house. The plant materials were chosen to meet functional needs, enhance the architecture, and provide seasonal interest. All of it, says Fein, meant to create an outdoor environment that expresses the house's midcentury style and creates outdoor rooms that unify the house and garden.

LEFT Freestanding privacy panels define garden areas that can be considered outdoor rooms, giving an opportunity to design a space that can be enjoyed as views from inside as well.

OPPOSITE, LEFT A *Cedrus atlantica* 'Glauca Pendula' brings greenery into the heart of a patio and hot tub area.

OPPOSITE, CENTER Pavers edged with rounded stones and forest grasses lead to a venue for private enjoyment of outdoor space outside a bedroom.

OPPOSITE, RIGHT From the interior, the efficacy of the privacy panels becomes evident; the clerestory windows allow additional views of the leafy tree canopy beyond.

LOS BONITOS

JOHNSON & D'AGOSTINO, AND AND AND STUDIO / TERREMOTO

LOS ANGELES, CALIFORNIA

The design for this midcentury house makes the most of mature trees and enhances the landscape

OPPOSITE Paving, furnishings, and pots are all kept light so as not to detract from the restored midcentury architecture. Plantings are also placed away from doors to facilitate unimpeded circulation (the columnar euphorbia is tucked into a corner just under the eaves), while groupings of plants are carefully placed to be enjoyed as views from the interior (the blooms of the *Pedilanthus bracteatus* are clearly visible as a colorful focal point from the kitchen).

This Los Feliz Estates house built in 1963 had a solid landscape context. "And," says Terremoto principal David Godshall, "it has always been our desire to be respectful and kind." In this case, there were what he termed "established and robust trees" to work with, along with much more.

The house itself was designed by the Los Angeles firm of Johnson & D'Agostino with a sawtooth roof and a sunken dining room, and in keeping with aspirations of the era and the postwar architectural spirit of Los Angeles, it embraced indoor-outdoor living.

The original owners had stayed true to its midcentury origins, but of course, decades later it showed both its age and the stylistic preferences of the previous (and original) occupants. After the current owners bought it, they hired the architecture and interior design firm of And And And Studio, who in turn, stripped it down to its bones and brought it back in a way that emphasized its midcentury allure.

The landscape needed less tampering. The house not only had the beginnings of a strong landscape but there was what Godshall calls "a through line" in terms of the intact indigenous and native plants on the site. Terremoto's approach was to make the landscape somehow seem like it was always so, "to thoughtfully and elegantly blur the edges," providing a soft and appealing gradient between the firm's design and what was always there.

Terremoto planted a single specimen tree, a fiddlehead fig that is visible from both inside and out. One goal of the design was to integrate house and garden in a way that the two seem almost symbiotic; the views into the house reflect the plants and trees outside, and it's almost impossible to envision the approach to the front door without its gallery of cacti and succulents.

For the most part, Terremoto opted for a mix of what Godshall calls "architectural cacti," succulents, and Mediterranean plants—all of them low or almost no water. The plants were selected both for ecological and architectural reasons. The color palette relies intentionally on greens and blues to complement the minimalism of the house. "It was," says Godshall, "more about sculpting space and complementing the architecture. "We didn't want to maximalize the landscape, but rather layer the plants to create an architectural experience."

LEFT *Yucca rostrata* and *Senecio mandraliscae* are variations on blue-toned, spiky themes.

OPPOSITE On the back patio, plants are chosen with golden-to-red accents or tones; these seem to catch and reflect the California sun.

LEFT The plantings were chosen to emphasize the color of the front door, and to create an architectural progression toward it; the organic shapes of the ground covers and low heights of the plants embellish the approach without overwhelming the house's clean lines.

OPPOSITE The defined shapes of the cacti, ground cover, yucca, vining shrubs, and grasses are each called into sharp relief by the strong sun. Slightly asymmetrical pavers add interest without distracting from the house's clean lines.

CHATEAU

LADD & KELSEY / TERREMOTO, KARA HOLEKAMP AND SAM WEBB

LOS ANGELES, CALIFORNIA

Small garden rooms open a beautifully sited house up to a panoramic vista

OPPOSITE A dining area surrounded by verdure, at eye height courtesy of Western redbuds (*Cercis occidentalis*), and at ground level *Lomandra longifolia* and *Myrtus compactus*.

In their day, the midcentury architects Ladd & Kelsey stood out among their counterparts for their adherence to a more Bauhaus-based European modernism in a region that had become known for its own design aesthetic. As a result, the firm, which was based in Pasadena, achieved less lasting fame than many of their California counterparts. Nonetheless, their work, which included the Pasadena Museum of Art and the Norton Simon Museum, has had an enduring presence in Southern California. A catalog entry in a 2019 exhibition devoted to their work commented that the firm's work was: "more elegant in style and formal in rigor than what was culturally popular at midcentury."

This particular house was built by the firm for architect-partner John Kelsey's own family and as such, it was conceived as a laboratory and showcase for his own ideas. It interweaves architecture and nature in a way that is both artistic and pragmatic—notably, it wraps around a sixty-six-foot-long swimming pool.

Terremoto's approach in redesigning the outdoor space was to create a series of small rooms close to the house, and to conceive a water-wise garden that layered textures, geographies, stories, and worlds. A sunny front garden juxtaposes silver and burgundy, with oaks and agaves, sycamores, and lavender. A more introspective, shadier courtyard garden to the interior balances lusher foliage with chaparral species.

The smaller garden rooms—a key concept drawn from modern garden design—give way to a more profuse and wilder landscape. Pasadena's location at the edge of the San Gabriel Mountains means that it has a much more untouched ecological base with wide and diverse offerings of native plants. Terremoto made good use of this as the landscape moves away from the house. The garden becomes almost ethereal, blurring the boundaries between the domestic realm of the home site and the natural world beyond.

LEFT, ABOVE The garden is a play on textures at every level; here a gravel-and-stone path is lined with *Thymus serpyllum* and *Stachys byzantina*.

LEFT *Verbena bonariensis* cheerfully pops up along a gravel path that traverses the changing grade and contours of the sloped site.

OPPOSITE A play on burgundies and purples as well as broad leaves and succulents. The pointed leaves of a *Platanus racemosa*, at left, receive an unexpectedly pleasurable echo in the form of the *Agave attenuata*, at right.

LEFT This outdoor room is readily accessible through sliding-glass doors, adding to the overall living space. Plants including *Cussionia spicata*, *Kalanchoe beharensis*, and a columnar euphorbia function as sculpture while erigeron acts as a plush carpet below.

ABOVE Waterwise gardens can provide plenty of lush and intriguing textures and colors if the movement of the seasons is also embraced; here the seed heads of *Phlomis purpurea* continue to add form to a backdrop of lavender and grasses.

OPPOSITE A path winds through a garden room filled with a riot of textures provided by *Aloe hercules*, the amazing seed cones of *Echium candicans* 'Pride of Madeira', *Lavandula heterophylla*, and the red-tipped *Leucadendron galpinii* 'Carlin'.

RUSTIC CANYON HOUSE

KARI RICHARDSON / MTLA

SANTA MONICA, CALIFORNIA

In Santa Monica, a once-ordinary house is transformed into a worldly paradise complete with an outdoor shower

OPPOSITE The design team decided on a cast-in-place stair to mediate the sloped site; it's filled in with Del Rio pea gravel. A *Cercis canadensis* 'Forest Pansy' anchors the foreground.

Mark Tessier had already done one garden for Matt Seaver and Will Speck, but then they called to say they'd found a new house. "Actually," Tessier recalls, "what they said was the house is totally ordinary but the land is spectacular." It backed up to a creek running through Santa Monica's Rustic Canyon, and, says Tessier, "it was a magical spot." There was one spectacular sycamore tree close to the house, almost too close—so much so that its visual impact was diminished, Tessier worried.

The site was filled with overgrown trees, bamboo, and ivy, and there was plenty of brick and concrete. Previous owners had basically ignored the gift of terrain the site had given them; the sloping lot had been graded to be a flat pad and you had to climb down steps to get to the creek. Tessier, whose Santa Monica–based landscape architecture firm is MTLA, carved into the land to return it to its natural grade and removed "that intimidating set of stairs." In the remodel by architect Kari Richardson, all the doors in the house were replaced with sliders so that basically, Tessier says, the front gate (made from reclaimed wood) essentially becomes the front door and the house and landscape work as a single living environment. "The boundaries of the living space are, functionally, the outer perimeters of the property," he says. There's even an outdoor shower that is used regularly.

Through the gate are front steps leading up to the house. They are concrete, but most of the paths are gravel, "so you get that crunchy sound beneath your feet," he says. Tessier opted for climatically appropriate plants sourced from Australia, South Africa, and throughout the Mediterranean to create a butterfly-friendly and lush landscape that has separate "landing pads" and outdoor rooms. And as for the sycamore tree that he worried was too near the house, "I solved it," Tessier says. "I simply attached it to the house with a deck so it became part of it."

LEFT This gate functions as the "front door" to the entire property. It's made of reclaimed wood from the site's original midcentury house and frames a mature sycamore.

OPPOSITE, LEFT An ipe deck and floating seating platform place focus, and therefore direct gratitude, toward the existing sycamore; midcentury-style garden chairs continue the period-appropriate theme throughout this patio area.

OPPOSITE, RIGHT Climate-adapted plants appear through the garden, including natives as well as those from Australia, South Africa, and the Mediterranean. Here California lilac acts as ground cover, along with a silver mountain flax.

OPPOSITE, LEFT A melaleuca tree seems to sprout directly from the path that connects the parking area to the main entry. Coast woollybush and meadow grasses, including *Leymus condensatus* 'Canyon Prince' and *Carex tumulicola* act as a buffer between the path and house.

OPPOSITE, RIGHT Verdant walls of foliage reach out along this side path, a match for the moody blue hue of the house.

RIGHT An area the owners call the "Discovery Meadow" fills in a slope in front of the house's lower level. Native *Carex tumulicola* and coast woollybush fill in, with a *Cercis canadensis* 'Forest Pansy' adding a pop of color in the background.

BACK AT THE RANCH

NEW GARDENS THAT ELEVATE AMERICA'S MOST POPULAR, UBIQUITOUS (AND OFTEN-MALIGNED) HOUSE

A few years back, some of Cliff May's ranch houses reached high peaks of acclaim. Occupants of small "Spanish stuccos" (an architectural phrase that followed the nondescript "California bungalow") were entranced with the long, low, look of the Cliff May house. "The feeling of weight and coolness," wrote James Toland in the *Los Angeles Times* in 1969, in an article that grudgingly said, essentially, "this is the best we have right now, till something better comes along."

Toland was commenting on the publication of Cliff May's book, *Western Ranch Houses*. By then May had widespread recognition as the father of the California ranch house, which quickly became the architectural standard, if not the model for country-wide mass-production. And it should be noted that the newspaper columnist's reluctant acceptance of the American ranch house might have come a bit too late; by then millions upon millions of Americans lived in ranch houses, though not all of them designed with the same level of care as May's.

In the year 1955, American homebuilders broke ground on more than 1,650,00 houses. Of these, ninety percent (which is to say almost a million and a half houses) were low-slung, one-story structures, which—though varied in finish, roof slope (or no slope), finish, and orientation—were considered to be ranch houses. That trend continued:

in the next four years alone, another six million ranch houses were built. Most of them, suffice it to say, had nothing to do with ranches.

The California, or Western, ranch house occupied a special place in this firmament, thanks primarily to May and his fierce devotion to the ideas of indoor-outdoor living. His Pace-Setter House, designed at the behest of *House Beautiful* editor Elizabeth Gordon, helped secure May a national reputation, and secure coast-to-coast attention and admiration for his designs. But its virtues were spread far and wide by the developers of suburban subdivisions and housing prototypes built by local contractors or by plan. A number of well-known architects and landscape architects participated in these efforts, from Charles M. Goodman at Hollin Hills in Virginia (where the public landscape came from Dan Kiley) to A.D. Stenger in Austin to William Krisel's Alexander Homes in Palm Springs. An array of architects designed Joseph Eichler's many homes, starting with Anshen & Allen but also including Raphael Soriano, Edward H. Fickett, and A. Quincy Jones, among many others, and some Eichler communities boasted public landscapes designed by Garrett Eckbo. East or West, ranch houses were omnipresent in the 1950s and 1960s.

EXPERIMENTAL RANCH

CLIFF MAY, MARMOL RADZINER / MARMOL RADZINER

LOS ANGELES, CALIFORNIA

A new landscape preserves and enhances a seminal midcentury designer's own iconic home

OPPOSITE The heavily-wooded original site featured desirable mature sycamores and oaks; the landscape architects added shade-tolerant natives to help the house integrate with the landscape as Cliff May likely originally intended.

In 1969, a reporter for the *Los Angeles Times* toured Cliff May's own house in Los Angeles, terming it "without doubt the best example of his work. Not the biggest nor the costliest, but the most personal and the most active, a kind of structural organism that has grown and altered and matured through its fifteen years."

The Experimental Ranch was the Brentwood house that May—the father of the California ranch house and more commonly referred to by his first name, as Cliff—lived in from 1952 almost until his death in 1989. May designed the house to be open (only the bathrooms were fully enclosed) and filled with light, thanks to a skylight that ran the length of the house as well as glass gables.

May's seminal book, *Western Ranch Houses*, sets forth four tenets of ranch house design: that it hugs the ground, is built of natural materials, fosters indoor-outdoor living, and has a "corridor: original family room." His own house provided a laboratory for exploring those ideas. The house, also known as Mandalay and widely covered in magazines across the country, had a one-thousand-square-foot living room with terraces at both ends and nine distinct outdoor living spaces. "It was the was the omega to his earlier alpha," wrote Daniel Gregory, author of a fine book on May. "And omega it was in terms of scale, design innovation, and gadgetry, because Cliff was Cliff, and this new house had to be more dramtic, eye-catching, and inventive than anything he had done before."

The master bedroom and living room both open onto terraces. A fifteen-foot sliding glass wall allows the central living space to extend into an adjoining terrace, or outdoor room. A primary feature of the architecture is a 288-square-foot skylight that punctuates the central gable of the home's low-pitched shingle roof and frames the tree canopies above. The skylight was originally designed to open and close automatically with fluctuating interior temperatures.

The original landscape was done by May's friend, the influential Thomas Church. ("My best houses have all been done with him," May once said.) Decades later, the multifaceted Los Angeles design firm (architects, landscape architects, furniture designers, and more) of Marmol Radziner took on the renovation and relandscaping of the more than half-century-old house, inside and out.

"When we began the project, there were old sycamores and oaks on the property, along with a few non-native trees, which we removed from the site. The garden was a mix of

shade-tolerant flowering shrubs like azaleas and camellias. The site gently slopes downward toward the seasonal creek. A hill rises behind the house," recalls one of the firm's design partners, Ron Radziner.

Marmol Radziner set out to preserve the native species that were on the site and supplement them with shade-tolerant natives. Then, "where native species do not fit the bill, we incorporate Mediterranean planting," says Radziner. The goal was to design "a visually compelling landscape that would draw the eye outward."

LEFT May's original beams and rafters lead the eye to floor-to-ceiling windows and the hillside beyond. Newly poured terrazzo floors integrate the interior with the natural materials outside.

OPPOSITE One of the house's most notable features is a skylight that spans the length of the great room living space, designed to allow appreciation of the high tree canopy above while inside.

RIGHT A fountain reminiscent of Italian Renaissance predecessors cascades down a slope while stone steps allow access for viewing native plants close up.

OPPOSITE, LEFT AND RIGHT Simple square pavers arranged in a subtle pattern provide firm footing for patio furniture; the intentional gaps between them provide space for greenery to invade the outdoor living room.

MALAGA HOUSE

THOMAS TRIPLETT RUSSELL, BRILLHART ARCHITECTURE / CARLOS SOMOZA

MIAMI, FLORIDA

In the junglelike setting of Miami's Coconut Grove neighborhood, a new landscape reinforces the power of reductive architecture

OPPOSITE Preserving the site's existing mature trees was as much a focus of the architectural renovations as protecting the 1948 house's midcentury spirit. The two-story addition is designed to float up into the canopy. The pavers are edged with *Aechmea chantinii* 'Green' and 'Black' bromeliads.

Miami's midcentury architects drew from the precedents set by others working elsewhere in America but adapted their houses to meet the demands of Florida's hot temperatures and profuse sunlight. The houses were, often, small and even modest, with cross ventilation and clerestory windows to let the light in and the heat out. The architects Jacob and Melissa Brillhart tackled the often-unforgiving job of more than tripling the size of an untouched 1948 case-study-inspired house by the Miami modernist Thomas Triplett Russell and met the challenge without changing the architecture of the original. That house, a low-slung "tropical modern" one-story ranch, was not a designated landmark, but the Brillharts carefully renovated it to preserve its character—this made possible by the addition of a new two-story glass-and-steel wing that is essentially beside and behind the original, leaving space for a new garden. Enter landscape architect Carlos Somoza.

When Somoza first encountered the site, it was more or less tabula rasa—limestone gravel and a "developer spec pool" surrounded by grass. A single sprawling *Ficus aurea* (Florida strangler fig) tree and a scattering of noteworthy trees—among them live oak, mango, and sea grape—had been left on the site. Says Somoza: "A steep slope separated the concrete promenade and the swimming pool. The developer did not provide any exterior living spaces or a transition from the upper promenade to the lower garden area. There is a thirty-foot grade change from the top of pool coping elevation to the concrete promenade that connects the kitchen, living room and bedroom areas."

One goal was to create a landscape that would offer a seamless transition from the interior to the exterior. Another to create a landscape that would enhance the indigenous landscape in this case by "using long horizontal lines that transverse through lush tropical plantings to provide the sensation that the garden is encroaching upon man-made elements." Here, stepping-stone pathways using architectural precast stone pavers cross through specimen palms, hardwood

4150

trees, bold-leafed philodendrons, and "large swaths of flowering perennials and groundcovers."

There are three separate outdoor living areas: a courtyard garden with the ficus (forty feet tall and forty feet in diameter) in the center, an upper terrace of Brazilian hardwood shaded by the big tree, and the lower pool area, all created by Somoza's firm along with engineers, builders, woodcrafters, horticulturalists, and an arborist. The pool was renovated and a waterfall added to create, Somoza says, "a tranquil sheet of water visible from the living spaces that surround the courtyard garden." Then he went to work on the actual garden. "My gardens often provide the illusion that the building and exterior spaces were carved out from a veritable jungle. I believe mystery and the element of surprise are among a landscape architect's most useful tools."

RIGHT Plantings along the house's original set of ribbon windows are kept low so as not to detract from the architectural line. Precast pavers enhance the horizontality while bromeliads, philodendrons, and flowering perennials wrap the building's exterior walls.

OPPOSITE The entry garden includes dense planting of palms and Caribbean natives meant to make the house appear as if it's in the middle of a jungle, all tucked behind a new Brazilian hardwood fence. *Hemigraphis alternata* features prominently as a dramatic ground cover.

OPPOSITE Specimen palms and hardwood trees provide height while *Calliandra haematocephala* 'Nana' attracts hummingbirds and *Myrcianthes fragrans* attracts cardinals and honeybees at mid-level in this subtropical garden.

ABOVE The two-story steel-and-glass addition features floor-to-ceiling windows to allow views from the new master suite, living areas, and second-floor bedrooms; the latter, in particular, were designed to evoke a feeling of living in a treehouse.

RIGHT An ipe-wood platform cantilevers around the site's most sacred plant, a 40-foot *Ficus aurea*, to protect its root system while allowing use of the space. Modern, large-format pavers update the newly installed pool, all surrounded by a collection of epiphytic orchids, bromeliads, and staghorn ferns.

SUNSWEPT DRIVE

BARBARA BESTOR / ELYSIAN LANDSCAPES

LOS ANGELES, CALIFORNIA

A renovation of a 1940s ranch house and a new landscape let it reclaim the grandeur of its setting

OPPOSITE Interior living spaces open doubly wide and directly onto a patio and lawn. Cactuses and agaves provide height and shape in the foreground, tempered by the soft tufts of *Pennisetum orientale*.

The house, as Barbara Bestor first encountered it, was a missed opportunity—a nondescript 1940s ranch house without many of the assets of the midcentury architectural style. Instead of open rooms, it had series of tight spaces, and it was, she says, "closed off from any views. It had very low ceilings, an enclosed porch, and small rooms." She completely remodeled it to have a large kitchen and an open-space plan, even to the point of raising the roof one-and-a-half feet and reconfiguring the house so that the master bedroom, main living space and a new porch all focused on the long view that stretches to the distant mountains.

Landscape designer Judy Kameon of Elysian Landscapes knew the homeowners from a previous project. "We wanted the indoor and outdoor experiences to feel seamlessly connected," she says. "We strived to create spaces that they could use for entertaining, recreation, dining, cooking, growing food, and overall enjoyment and enhancement of their daily lives."

Kameon opted for an "eclectic mix" of California natives and low-water Mediterranean and subtropical trees, plants, and shrubs. She followed a specific color palette that was in sync with the interior (it is neutral and blues) to reinforce the seamless connection between indoors and out. "We selected a range of foliage colors that included a lot of metallic tones, such as silver, bronze, gold, and black, coupled with floral accents of lavender and blue," she says. "Grasses and strappy foliage were partnered with cactus and succulents to soften and highlight their sculptural forms."

As a sister company to Elysian Landscapes, Kameon also designs furniture under her Plain Air label. She designed a built-in outdoor bed off the living room. Plain Air also designed or selected the freestanding outdoor furniture for the project. And she says, "We rounded out the spaces with pots, a water feature and hanging lights in the pergola. Every detail was considered!"

The siting of the house offered an opportunity to create a foreground, middle ground, and a long vista. "Rather than press everything up against the house, we pushed some spaces out into the garden to activate the overall landscape, like the firepit area and the teepee," says Kameon. "We felt it was important to provide shade close to the house so that the outdoor spaces we created there could be used year-round." To this end, she designed was an expansive pergola that runs along the back of the house. "We carefully framed the existing views of the mountains and borrowed landscape to maintain open vistas, balanced with dense vegetation at the perimeter to create a sense of privacy and enclosure."

LEFT A natural gray concrete patio is shaded by a steel pergola with a retractable canvas awning. Capiz shell globe fixtures tie into a low-voltage lighting system, softly illuminating both a minamalist tile-top dining table set by Plain Air and a built-in upholstered daybed.

OPPOSITE A small seating area is framed by plants including *Cercidium* 'Desert Museum', *Phormium* 'Black Adder', and silver-toned succulents and perennials to provide privacy while keeping sightlines open to the view. The meadow grass in the foreground is an alternative to sod. The hoop chairs and steel firepit filled with black lava rock are by Plain Air, and sit on a decomposed granite patio.

NADER HOUSE

BARBARA BESTOR / ANA SAAVEDRA

LOS ANGELES, CALIFORNIA

In capable hands, a ranch house in the Los Angeles foothills becomes an artful and colorful work of architecture and nature

OPPOSITE Plantings in horizontal bands accentuate the long lines of the one-story ranch house. Whimsical tufts of zoysia grass lead to rows of agaves, succulents, and two small trees espaliered to accentuate the otherwise-unbroken plane of an exterior wall, which in turn highlight the canary-yellow front door.

When the architect Barbara Bestor first encountered this house it was, she says, "semi-abandoned and leaking. It was not in very good shape." Still, she and her client, Miriam Nader, the television writer and creator of the hit series *Two Broke Girls,* saw the potential and forged ahead. "We loved the bones of the existing house, including dramatic clerestory windows that are now cleaned and revealed," she says.

Bestor added the landscape designer Ana Saavedra (along with Cy and Genevieve Carter of Carter Design for the interiors) to create a house that embraces the extraordinary natural light in Los Angeles and opens up to the outdoors. The interior, says Bestor, originally had numerous small rooms that were not connected to the view and were thus very dark. Bestor's team had to "completely reshuffle" the interior spaces, opening up the central core of the house. The architects created a spacious open kitchen with a shaded dining area just outside. Bestor kept the original sunken living room but better connected it to the backyard so that it would be infused with natural light. The master bedroom, likewise, opens to the landscape. The pool was added.

Landscape designer Saavedra was, at the time, working with Bestor on another project just five doors down the street and already well understood "Barbara's vision in the relationship between building and garden, her unique design approach. Our client, Michelle Nader, has an eye for art and color—you see it throughout the house. She wanted drought tolerant, clean, contemporary, and pops of color, just like her art adorning the interiors." Saavedra developed an overall strategy that worked seamlessly with the architecture, using plants as an art form.

She chose both Mediterranean and desert plants, largely to meet the requirements of a good deal of sun and much less water. But by grouping them she began to develop a palette "with a base of blue and true green colors accentuated by hints of red and yellow." Though the plants originated in different ecosystems, they relate to each other in terms of water requirements, sun patterns, soil types, or habitat.

The site of the house offered its own artistry: "great wind and sun and shade patterns that I wanted to visually bring into the interior experience of the garden," she says. To capitalize on this, she installed such plants as *Rhodocoma capensis* (the South African cape restio), planted at the base of the doors and windows, "to allow for their soft plume-like foliage and the wind movement to be visually part of the interiors." Likewise, just outside the kitchen window there is a giant planter of *Philodendron selloum*, which Saavedra says "is a very old-school, common plant, but in this case Michelle wanted something green and massive that was exciting and exuberant as a single element."

In the front yard, the Korean grass lawn (a true green, clumping form) offers a visual contrast with the soft, low mounds of blue *Artemisia* 'Powis Castle', and both are juxtaposed against the architectural blue agaves and taller blue soft *Acacia covenyi*, *Aloe arborescens*, and an evergreen mass of *Lomandra longifolia*.

"In true Bestor signature," says Saavedra, this is the house with the only bright-yellow door in the neighborhood. It is artfully bold and unapologetic, so to honor that we found two great ginkgo espaliers that were planted on one side of the door as an homage to Michelle and her son, Bruno. "The ginkgos, the only vertical element on the front facade, arc truc green color in summer, then turn "this amazing bright yellow color in fall" before becoming a bare, pure structure in winter. "It's very artful," says Saavedra.

"We wanted to bring bright and sunny back," says Bestor. "The client also loves color and did not want the house to be stark white. We wanted to create a bright, lively, lived-in palette for the family."

RIGHT The designer included Australian and South African species in this waterwise garden, including a large leucadendron to add subtle reddish purples to the landscape.

OPPOSITE A fiddle-leaf fig acts as sentry, while blooming aloes add a pop of red to complement the succulents' blue hues.

ABOVE AND RIGHT In true 1960s midcentury ranch indoor/outdoor style, the back patio can be accessed from numerous rooms. A pergola with a retractable shade shields the dining area from intense sunlight, while air plants whimsically dot the far wall. The small expanse of lawn is appreciated by the owner's teenage son.

SPORTS LOVER'S HIDEAWAY

KLOPF ARCHITECTURE / STUDIO M MERGE

LOS GATOS, CALIFORNIA

A decades-long project produced a mecca for an active family that also loves the peaceful experience of nature

OPPOSITE Variations on shaggy greens provide intriguing texture while keeping the overall palette of this yard simple for visual harmony.

This is a house that speaks to collaboration and to the yin and yang of modern architecture. The mandate for the architects and landscape architects was not simple: to create a house that could and would brim over with activity, from swimming laps to shooting hoops and embracing the active life, and to create a garden conducive to quiet moments of contemplation.

Over the course of a decade, the architects and landscape architects transformed what John Klopf said was a "typical midcentury house" into one that not only fulfilled the owners' dreams but also showcased the true possibilities of the modernist ethos of connecting architecture and nature by opening the house to the landscape.

As is often the case in design, John Klopf affirmed that, "In many ways, it was more about the experience of the daylight and the experience of creating the space." The architect is widely regarded as a leading expert in the renovation of midcentury architecture, especially (but not limited to) Eichler houses; his own contemporary work also invokes both the stylistic and philosophical principles of the period.

The first phase of the assignment was to design a pool house that would be sited orthogonally to the pool and frame the long view afforded by the adjacent golf course, giving the owners, said Klopf, "a unique view of nature." That was followed, in stages, by the addition of an attached ADU (additional dwelling unit) that could double as a sports bar as well as expand the interior spaces and open up the view, "taking the original ideas of the midcentury period and expanding upon them," he says.

The landscape mandate, said Andrea Sessa of M Merge, was to reorganize the open space, transforming the lawns with "a very calm, limited palette—nothing flashy." Later the architects added a raised deck and expanded both the interior space and the view into the front greenery as well as the golf course beyond. "It was not about creating an object to look at," Klopf said.

The landscape itself is anchored by mature oak and redwood trees, as well as maples and enough paper birches to "make a grove," said Sessa. The palette is primarily various shades of green "with lush grasses" offset by blue, but all very subtle and subdued. "Everything is filtered," said Sessa, "and imparts a sense of calm." And it is this that becomes the background for exuberant gatherings.

ABOVE Geometric tufts of grasses make the path to the door clear at ground level, while at eye level and in the upper canopy, silvery greens and tree leaves catch the California sunlight.

OPPOSITE Broad paths make circulation easy between the plunge pool and basketball and horseshoe courts while low plantings of various textures create distinct rooms within the garden but allow open sightlines..

LAZENBY RESIDENCE

MARK HAMPTON / RAYMOND JUNGLES

SOUTH MIAMI, FLORIDA

In South Miami, a simple house becomes dramatic with a lush, artistic, and colorful tropical landscape

OPPOSITE Mature live oaks and a mahogany near the front entry were some of the only plants retained; their leaves now cast playful shadows on concrete pavers below, pressed with rock salt for texture, while staghorn ferns nestle in the crooks of their branches.

The Miami architect Mark Hampton's career began in the midcentury and spanned more than five decades. In this project, the renovation of a 1960s ranch house in South Miami, he asked the landscape architect Raymond Jungles to join him in transforming a plain, dull space into a tropical retreat that connected house and garden, making them one, and celebrated the potential of the beneficial warm and sunny climate. The garden offers a play of scale and texture, using plants selected for their form and their color as both sculpture and architecture.

There were mature oaks on the site, as well as a single mahogany tree near the front door, all worth keeping. But Jungles relocated the driveway, which had been uncomfortably close to the front door, to create "a sense of ceremony and arrival," and then, in another reminder that this is Florida, covered the driveway with sand rather than asphalt because the driveway is shaded by the oaks. A series of elevated, textured concrete platforms—the concrete was formed with rock salt impressions to create a more naturalistic surface—lead to a deck underneath the mahogany tree.

Jungles moved the swimming pool, creating spaces for outdoor entertaining that include areas for barbecuing and for dining, all connected with the interior kitchen and living room. The old swimming pool became a fountain—he terms it a "bubbling water element"—that not only soothes and pleases but helps mitigate the exposure to noise and traffic on this corner lot. Careful consideration was given to the views from the house to the garden, day and night, and vice versa.

LEFT A *Platycerium bifurcatum* finds a new home in the branches of a *Quercus virginiana*. Groupings of *Neomarica gracilis* and *Aechmea* 'Dean' bromeliads add lushness at ground level. The drive is paved with sand for permeability.

OPPOSITE Asymmetric poured-in-place concrete pavers with a warm tone lead to the main entry. *Ophiopogon japonicus* 'Nana' fills the gaps between, while palms *Chamberyonia macrocarpa*, *Heterospathe elata*, and *Satakentia liukiuensis* conceal the house from the road.

ABOVE The infinity edge of the pool laps over a stacked stone wall, providing the aural effects of a water feature.

RIGHT An accent wall of travertine and ipe wood adds a moment of sculpture and architecture to the decadently tropical plantings that surround it.

LEFT A *Heliconia caribaea* 'Yellow' marks the entry to a path through dense plantings of *Philodendron* 'Burle Marx' and *Heliconia* 'Pedro Ortiz'.

OPPOSITE No Tropical Modern property would be complete without palms; this *Heterospathe elata* was added to the pool deck to add a curved dimension to the otherwise highly recilinear organization of the architecture and yard.

INTO THE WOODS

WHEN THE MIDCENTURY GARDEN MEETS NATURE

Not quite an hour outside New York City lies the former home of Russel and Mary Wright, Manitoga, built on an abandoned quarry site near the town of Garrison. At first blush, it may seem to be nature untouched—or at least, less touched—but in fact it is a carefully orchestrated and fully modern woodland landscape that offers many lessons in both ecology and design. In recent years, this landscape—the Wrights bought the seventy-five-acre site in 1942—has been scrutinized, studied, and carefully tended. Though Russel Wright may be best remembered for his design of the extraordinary American Modern dinnerware, both he and Mary were multifaceted designers whose view of what could be modern ranged from the smallest salad fork to the broad, rocky acreage where they built their house.

"Wright's house is built alongside the cliffs of an old quarry and it clings to the rugged terrain as if nature had planned the setting for the wood and glass structure," wrote Gay Pauley. "Actually, Wright said when he gave us a tour of the home, he rearranged nature extensively. He diverted a stream so it would spill into the quarry to form a waterfall and swimming pool as deep as twenty feet in some places. He also rearranged some of the outcroppings of rock, with the help of a derrick, block and tackle, construction crew, and local stonemasons. Birch, hemlock and other trees were cleared to expose the jagged vertical quarry walls, which, if you use your imagination, create the shape of a dragon." Thus the name given it by then-eleven-year-old Annie Wright, "Dragon Rock."

That house alone speaks volumes about modernism and landscape. The Wrights worked with the architect David Leavitt over the course of nineteen years to complete the project.

Across the country, another Wright—Frank Lloyd Wright (no relation)—had become inarguably the most famous architect in the land, particularly for Fallingwater in Mill Run, Pennsylvania, which was inextricable from its setting. In those years, Richard Neutra was the second-most-famous architect in the land, and his philosophy and architecture were even more intertwined with natural settings. Russel Wright had equal fame—he was the designer of the most popular dinnerware in America—but he was a designer whose work reached a far more common, popular denominator, which set him apart.

He also set a new paradigm for the incorporation of nature and architecture (and vice versa). Wrote Pauley, who was of course a contemporary observer walking through the house with Wright: "Nature is brought inside every room in the form of laminated butterfly, leaf, and flower panels; in hemlock needles embedded in green plaster walls; in the sound of the waterfall heard in every room; in the giant fireplace in the living room formed with native stone of all sizes; in the weathered oak beams treated only with a preservative in the stone steps and floor of the two-level living room, and the in the single spire of rugged red cedar trunk, two stories tall, which supports the major beam of the main house."

Wright's point of view shines through, and it is decidedly modernist—offering clarity and perspective. His order is not drawn from strict geometry but more from an organic view of the way nature could and should unfold as it's experienced.

MENDEL RESIDENCE

SCRAFANO ARCHITECTS / MARK TESSIER

SAN FERNANDO VALLEY, CALIFORNIA

A ranch house conjures up memories of the owner's childhood and creates new ones as well

OPPOSITE An ipe-wood bridge that pairs with the 1953 ranch house's updated cladding traverses a sunken garden of succulents and cape rush.

Nate Mendel grew up in the Pacific Northwest, where he was free to roam in the woods. But in the outskirts of often-parched Los Angeles, re-creating that experience—and in a responsible way—was a challenge. "There were only a few trees on the site," says the landscape architect Mark Tessier, principal of firm MTLA. He needed to build a forest, and to do this he needed trees, and a lot of them. Tessier went from nursery to nursery asking for the "all the old, unused unloved orphan sycamore trees. They were crooked, bent, leaning." But taken together, they built woods where there had been none.

The garden is conceived as a series of outdoor rooms compatible with the ranch house's design; there are spaces for nature, horticulture, agriculture, and play. There's a secret garden for adults and an adventure garden for children.

The house itself was a 1953 ranch with panoramic views of the Los Angeles Valley and in the distance, the Verdugo and San Gabriel Mountains. Scrafano modernized the house, adding metal roofs, and built a compatible but contemporary studio used by Mendel, a musician, that doubles as a guest house on the site.

The hardscape draws on the rectilinear lines of the architecture, basically zigzagging through the property in a modern interpretation of a more classical woodland garden. Where there is not forest, Tessier opted for what he terms "big fleshy plants," cactus and succulents. The family pool sits in a play lawn for the family, more like a "rug" of grass, Tessier says. To reach Mendel's studio, you must pass through a citrus grove of Valencia oranges, a nod to the region's agricultural past. The Mendel family picks and squeezes every orange, he says.

One problem Tessier and the renovation team from Scrafano confronted was that although it's a deep lot, the house sits close to the street. Tessier wanted to mitigate that by creating what he calls a "compression zone." To achieve this he planted a dense green hedge of evergreens and stone fruit trees, then behind the gate, created a sunken garden, "kind of a moat if you will," with a concrete water basin based on Japanese purification fountains and a feng shui–inspired bridge that is crossed on the way to the front door, a transition from the chaos outside.

RIGHT A paved patio on the same grade as the house facilitates indoor/outdoor movement for adults and children to access the play lawn. A Brazilian pepper tree is limbed up to retain shade without blocking views from the interior.

OPPOSITE, LEFT A geometric path of decomposed granite is a match for the rectilinear lines of the house's architecture. It traverses plantings of blue carex grass and woolly bush, all under native California sycamore.

OPPOSITE, RIGHT The infinity-edge fountain at the house's entry burbles to welcome visitors and is visible from inside the entry hall as well.

RIGHT Opting to keep the garden's color palette simple, the clients chose patio furniture cushions to match the color of the kniphofia in the foreground.

OPPOSITE A geometric orchard of a dozen organic orange trees harkens back to the area's agrarian past and provides an immersive, calming retreat while pairing well with the geometry of the rest of the property.

MIDDLE RIVER RESIDENCE

POWERSSCHRAM / CADENCE

FORT LAUDERDALE, FLORIDA

A family house on Fort Lauderdale's Middle River becomes a safe haven for creatures great and small

OPPOSITE The paving, with planting interspersed for permability, mimics the horizontal lines of the house's siding and was carefully installed around the specimen mahogany tree, now protected with a raised bed and given small bromeliads for company.

Though it is a sliver just larger than a third of an acre, this Fort Lauderdale landscape is a certified wildlife habitat, luring in birds and butterflies and bees—and the requisite four-legged creatures. (For sure, there are northern mockingbirds, blue jays, American white ibis, mottled ducks, red belly turtles, eastern gray squirrels, and iguanas—the last being tough on green matter, requiring "iguana resistant" plants at the water's edge.) When Rebecca Bradley and Gage Couch, principals of Cadence Landscape Architects of Fort Lauderdale, Florida, first encountered the site, they were struck by the profuse tree canopy there. "And we got to work within that tree canopy," says Couch.

The house was a typical midcentury Florida rambler with no discernible provenance; deep searches to find the name of an architect yielded nothing. The new owners—only the second owners of the house—assembled a team that included Cadence and the architectural firm of PowersSchram, which had temporarily relocated from Boston. "A lot of people would have torn the house down," says Bradley.

Because the house is comparatively small, this meant that the lot, which backs up to the Middle River in the center of Fort Lauderdale, seemed especially spacious. The designers kept the outdoor pool, which is well-used by the family of five and their two dogs, and they were able to save a specimen mahogany that is now the centerpiece of the house's entry courtyard as well as a showy seven-year apple tree. Many other native trees became the touchstones of this restored natural hammock, including, critically, black ironwood, native stopper, and bay cedar.

RIGHT Decades-old canopy trees that tower above the roofline are given the company of black ironwood and bay cedars to mediate height, and are underplanted with ferns, colocasia, and verdant ground cover to add interest along the perimeter wall.

OPPOSITE A new gate and a coat of paint refresh the original perimeter wall, which also dates to the 1950s.

RIGHT A low aqua accent wall in the backyard reflects the colors of the pool up and into the yard, a reinterpretation of the often-bold midcentury use of blocks of color in residences.

OPPOSITE The pool terrace provides views out to the river and access down to a lawn dotted playfully with circular pavers enjoyed by the family's three children. A multistory canopy of trees re-creates the landscape original to the area, prior to development.

DRY FALLS

WILLIAM KRISEL, DON BOSS / STEVE MARTINO

PALM SPRINGS, CALIFORNIA

A house in a dramatic setting pays homage to the sun-drenched beauty of the desert, its design enhanced by a bold use of color

OPPOSITE Yuccas, including the always-dramatic Spanish dagger (*Yucca faxoniana*) and palms tuck the house into a seeming oasis with the backdrop of the desert behind. Boulders and rocks anchor the garden in the mountainous region, while the golden hues of *Echinocactus grusonii* reflect the strong sunlight as well as the yellow entry wall behind.

The name Dry Falls derives directly from this house's dramatic setting—on a huge black rock outcropping that transforms into a waterfall if and when it rains. The house itself is part of an Alexander Homes subdivision and was designed by the Los Angeles architect William Krisel in 1957–58. For the most part there was little attention paid to the original landscapes in those developments, points out Steve Martino, because the buyers of these houses were in general interested in golf, which meant grass. But they also felt they should include the ubiquitous symbol of Southern California: palm trees.

And yet, Martino says, the house eventually named Dry Falls stands next to "this big, fantastic mountain" whose attributes weren't included in the house's visuals. It is the second landscape design he's done for this particular client. On the first, he says, he was "more timid," and retained remnants of the previous landscaping. "The second time, I took out all the remaining grass."

Though Martino, who lives and works in Tucson, Arizona, is a landscape architect by definition, his work transcends the narrower definitions of the field; he considers himself a garden designer, but one propelled by the idea that garden design is, or at least can be and ought to be, art. His work is at once horticultural and architectural, and he has been in the forefront of transforming the desert landscape ethos from one of water reliance and imported plants and trees to a drought-tolerant, low-water approach that embraces cacti and succulents including aloes, agaves, and yuccas, along with other native and well-adapted species such as ocotillo.

At Dry Falls, as with many of his projects, the results are dramatic. Krisel's Alexander house embraces the California sun, but in service to letting it stream in, left little consideration for privacy. Martino added plants in abundance to screen the interior living spaces and at the same time merge architecture with nature-making. He says his goal was to let "the inside

and the outside run together." Here, he adds, "the biggest room in the house is actually the backyard."

Martino's gestures are not necessarily subtle. He is unafraid of the bold use of color at a large scale—very much in the tradition of Luis Barragán. At Dry Falls, he's introduced a solid red wall as a backdrop to the pool and a foreground to the mountains; a goal of his work is to edit the views so that each vantage point "visually embraces something good." That means having every window act as a picture frame, and where the "painting" it frames changes continually as the sun creates shadows.

Dry Falls is a recent project in a long career, but in many ways offers a concise summary of Martino's deep knowledge of desert plants and kinship with the desert itself—one coupled with a strong sense of both landscape architecture and the principles of modernism.

LEFT Low, staggered, textured walls create privacy from the street and also enhance the shadows the desert sun casts as it changes throughout the day.

OPPOSITE A contemporary reflecting pool under the entry path brings the midcentury house into the twenty-first century while strategic lighting enhances the strikingly sculptural forms of the plants' tufty fronds, textured trunks, and architectural stems.

ABOVE A bold red wall in the tradition of Luis Barragán forms a bold backdrop for the backyard. The privacy wall is kept to a height that allows for another great tradition of desert developments to be preserved: borrowing the neighbors' view of swaying palms.

OPPOSITE Three *Aloe* 'Hercules' surround a vibrant yellow wall while a shorter, rounder aloe draws the eye to the right and barrel cactuses that look as though they might have just tumbled naturally down from the hills beyond edge a pool and patio set up for ultimate relaxation.

MANATUCK

MARYANN THOMPSON / REED HILDERBRAND

STONINGTON, CONNECTICUT

A new house draws on early modernism for its architectural precedents and digs deeper into history for its landscape

OPPOSITE A thickly planted shrub garden functions as perimeter wall to the contemporary house, reserving views out to the farmland beyond until visitors have entered and moved through the house. Its forms accentuate the architecture; remaining low under ribbon windows and accenting high solid walls by fronting them with sculptural trees.

A centuries-old farm had come up for sale, and there was a strong possibility that its fertile two hundred acres and another adjacent one hundred acres would be subdivided into as many as sixty housing sites. Barbara and Christopher Dixon stepped in, along with two sympathetic neighbors, to help save the land, which included Manatuck, the last remaining large farm in Stonington borough, and in so doing transformed it.

"The property is on North Main Street, which is the main thoroughfare between I-95 and Stonington Borough, a quintessential New England seaside village," says Barbara Dixon. "It's a rural road lined with old trees, stone walls, fields, and woods. The borough has beautiful examples of New England domestic architecture from the mid- to late-seventeenth century to the late nineteenth century. We saw no reason to build a replica."

The couple thought briefly about building a shingle-style house, but then reconsidered. "It was pretty clear that we needed to do something original, something contemporary, and because of this extraordinary site, and the history related to it, something fantastic," Barbara Dixon says.

A portion of this land was set aside as a conservation easement to preserve the open fields and glacial landforms in perpetuity. Then the Dixons built a modernist house on the working farm part of the land. The Dixons had worked with Doug Reed of the Cambridge, Massachusetts, and New Haven, Connecticut firm of Reed Hilderbrand on previous landscape projects. Reed, in turn, had worked extensively the architect Maryann Thompson, whose practice is in Watertown, Massachusetts. Together they created gardens and a landscape that spoke to the land's rich history but also fit effortlessly with the aesthetics and architectural idiom of the house.

The broad setting is pastures divided by historic New England stone walls, and the architects sited the house to nestle between two beech trees, its design intended not to overpower its surroundings but rather make it part of the "multiple readings" of the landscape. There are broad expanses of glass with sliding doors on the south and east facades that turn the house into an indoor-outdoor pavilion with indoor-outdoor rooms to frame the unobstructed view of the

ABOVE The rear of the house is organized to overlook a series of "viewing terraces." The first is defined by a massive granite foundation wall from a nineteenth-century barn. The property is the largest remaining parcel, at two hundred acres, in the area, allowing for the luxury of broad open spaces.

OPPOSITE Existing sycamore, beech, and elm trees are integrated into rebuilt historic stone walls from the original working farm, while the meadow grasses beyond leave the view out to Long Island Sound open.

farmland and, from a balcony off the master bedroom, of Long Island Sound in the distance. The farm is named Manatuck, which in the Algonquin language means "place of lookout."

The landscape offers a powerful look at history and a promising glimpse of the future. Reed honored the artifacts of the site—the patterns of walls, fields, and hedgerows. The landscape is organized along a six-hundred-foot-long ruined foundation wall of granite from a nineteenth-century barn that is, in places, twelve feet tall. For Reed, these visible artifacts tell the story of "hard work of generations of families and communities as they cultivated an economic and social system evolved from the fruits of the land."

The driveway climbs the drumlin—the long rolling glacial hill—from Stonington's North Main Street past hay fields. It is past the house that the panoramic view unfolds in a series of lawn terraces that open up the sight of farmland and woods and the water beyond. There are terraces, a pool, and vegetable and perennial gardens that connect to a system of fields, stone walls, and woodlands. Reed chose materials from a working agrarian landscape to reinforce the rural character, including Cor-Ten steel steps and retaining walls, galvanized metal agricultural fencing, and old stone collected on-site. To reinforce the existing mature trees (among them, sycamore, beech, and elm), Reed added swamp oaks, red oaks, and tulip trees. Because it has remains a working farm, the trees provide shade for the animals. The landscape contributes to the farm's sustainable agricultural practices of the Dixons as well as the farmers and gardeners who work on it, proving that a modernist landscape can be productive as well as functional.

LEFT Stones collected on site form an accent wall to either side of a reflecting pool, tying old and new elements together.

OPPOSITE Cor-Ten steel steps recall agricultural equipment of years past while defining a broad terrace. New trees added near the house include native swamp and red oaks and tulip trees.

LEFT Perennial plantings fill beds close to the house, while views out over the rolling drumlin/ravine landscape, now preserved as a conservation easement, are kept open.

OPPOSITE Architect and landscape architect collaborated closely to site the new house in relationship to the historic stone foundation wall and to nestle it into a bosque of existing and new trees to help it recede into the rolling hillside and to orchestrate a carefully planned entry sequence along the drumlin's slopes.

ACKNOWLEDGMENTS

This book has been a long journey, a process of exploration and discovery that began in 2017, which in retrospect seems not just seven years ago, but more like an epoch. There are many people to that, but at the top of the list is Stacee Gravelle Lawrence, who not only conceived the idea for this book but hung on through the roller-coaster ride of Covid, corporate change, and other upheavals but persevered and emerged as the founder of Cydonia Editions. Stacee has believed in it throughout. I also want to thank the many landscape architects who generously offered me not just their talents, patiently waited through the saga of making this book, and allowed me to take up too much of their time so all of us can enter the magical gardens they have created. I feel that especially now, as I am so attuned to looking at gardens, I regret that space and time (and more) made it impossible to show every superb garden I found along the way. I've long written about architecture and design and am more of a latecomer to the world of landscape architecture, but I am fully infatuated by it and look forward to exploring more the remarkable work of the sublimely talented garden designers I've already encountered and those I've yet to meet. My personal and unending gratitude goes to my many garden gurus (all of whom know vastly more than I do), including Margaret Doyle, Joanna Lombard, Patricia Lombard, Barbara Faga, and Rocco Ceo. Profound thanks go to my son, Adam Dunlop-Farkas, and his wife, Corinne Stikeman, who graciously put me up (and put up with me) during my several reconnaissance visits to Los Angeles. And on another personal note: ironically enough, three of the gardens featured in this book have connections to my alma mater, Vassar College; one was designed for a house built by the architect Margaret McCurry, who graduated just before my time there, and two others for my own classmates, who had the vision to commission fine gardens for their homes. Susan Henshaw Jones and her husband, Richard Eaton, hired Raymond Jungles to make her first Key West house into a tropical gem, a landscape I first encountered when I was on the jury that gave the national American Society of Landscape Architects award (and to be honest, I only learned it was hers some three or four years after the fact). The other landscape was commissioned by Barbara Saslaw Dixon, who died quite unexpectedly in 2023. Barbara was a great champion of landscape preservation and of conservation in the larger sense (as well as a board cochair of the Cultural Landscape Foundation, and the house (by Maryann Thompson) and landscape (by Doug Reed of Reed Hilderbrand) she and her husband, Chris Dixon, commissioned not only is a work of breathtaking beauty but sets a standard for preserving our too-often-endangered environment. In her honor (and in honor of the many astute clients and their equally amazing designers), I hope that in some small measure, this book will inspire others to preserve and enhance the legacy of midcentury modern living.

First published in the United States of America in 2025 by
Rizzoli International Publications, Inc.
49 West 27th Street
New York, NY 10001
www.rizzoliusa.com

Copyright © 2025 Beth Dunlop

All rights reserved. No part of this publication may be reproduced, stored in a retrieval system, or transmitted in any form or by any means, electronic, mechanical, photocopying, recording, or otherwise, without prior consent of the publishers.

Publisher: Charles Miers
Editor: Stacee Gravelle Lawrence
Design: John Clifford and Tim Littleton
Production Manager: Rebecca Ambrose
Managing Editor: Lynn Scrabis

ISBN: 978-0-8478-4692-4
Library of Congress Control Number: 2024947076

Printed in China
2025 2026 2027 2028 / 10 9 8 7 6 5 4 3 2 1

Visit us online:
Instagram.com/RizzoliBooks
Facebook.com/RizzoliNewYork
X: @Rizzoli_Books
Youtube.com/user/RizzoliNY

PHOTOGRAPHY CREDITS

© Peter Aaron/OTTO: 2, 65, 66, 67

© Caitlin Atkinson: 58, 60, 61, 62, 63, 118, 120, 121, 122, 123, 124, 126, 127, 128 left, 128 right, 129

© Birgitta Wolfgang Bjørnvad/The Sisters Agency: 138, 142 left, 142 right, 143

© Peter Bohler: 80 top

Courtesy Brillhart Architecture: 90

Steven Brooke: 166, 168, 169, 170, 171, 172, 173

© Robert Coscarelli: 35, 36 top, 36 bottom, 37, 38, 39

© Jack Coyier Photography: 79, 80 bottom, 81

© Roger Davies/OTTO: 45, 46, 47, 48, 49

Courtesy EPT Design: 72, 74, 75, 76, 77

© Joe Fletcher: 140, 141,

© Art Gray: 131, 132, 133 left, 133 right, 134 left, 134 right, 176, 178 left, 178 right, 179, 180, 181

© Bob Greenspan Photography: 115, 116, 117 all

© Steve Hall/Hedrich Blessing: 68, 70 top, 70 bottom, 71

© Millicent Harvey: 22, 24, 25, 50, 52, 53, 54, 55, 92, 94, 95, 96, 97, 98, 99, 189, 190, 191, 192, 193

© Laure Joliet: 152, 154, 155, 157, 158, 159, 160

Courtesy LGLA Landscape: 40, 41 top, 41 bottom, 43, 102, 104, 105, 106, 107

© Charles Mayer Photography: 20, 23

© Ngoc Minh Ngo: 194, 196, 197, 198, 199, 200, 201

© Lanny Provo Photography: 108, 110, 111, 112, 113

© Mariko Reed: 162, 164, 165

© Carlos Somoza: 145, 146, 147, 148, 150, 151

© Michael Stavaridis: 183, 184, 185, 186, 187

© Tim Street-Porter: 26, 28, 29, 30 left, 30 right, 31, 32, 33

© Trevor Tondro/OTTO: 161

Courtesy Word + Carr Design Group: 82, 84, 85, 86, 87

© Claudia Uribe: 88, 91

ABOUT THE AUTHOR

Beth Dunlop is one of the country's most noted architectural writers. She was the Pulitzer-nominated architecture critic for the *Miami Herald* for more than two decades, the editor of *Home Miami* magazine from 2007 to 2010, and of *Modern Magazine* from 2011 to 2017, and she is the author of numerous books including *Addison Mizner: Architect of Fantasy and Romance*, *Arquitectonica*, and *Florida's Vanishing Architecture*. Her writing has appeared widely in architecture, design, and travel magazines. She has won many awards including a medal for writing and criticism from the American Institute of Architecture. She lives in Miami Shores, Florida.